# RIDE

# RIDE

JOHN BUULTJENS

## BMX GLORY
### AGAINST ALL THE ODDS

WITH
## CHRIS SWEENEY

First published by Pitch Publishing, 2017

Pitch Publishing
A2 Yeoman Gate
Yeoman Way
Worthing
Sussex
BN13 3QZ

www.pitchpublishing.co.uk
info@pitchpublishing.co.uk

ISBN 978-1-78531-338-7

Typesetting and origination by Pitch Publishing

Printed in Great Britain by TJ International.

# Contents

*Dedicated to John's daughter,*
*Mackenzie Mae Buultjens.*

# Prologue

WHAT a ride.

I'm standing in Petaluma and can barely believe it.

It's a town in northern California.

Just even being here considering the start I had in life is enough.

I've been through stomach-churning domestic violence and a spell in an unforgiving children's home.

I've been mentally scarred and spent most of my youth completely consumed by rage.

But I'm here, on the set of a Hollywood movie – and to add to the madness, the entire thing is based on me and my life.

There are cameras whizzing by, booms swinging around and actors getting prepped in their trailers.

Chris 'Ludacris' Bridges, one of the stars of the *Fast and the Furious* film franchise, is playing the man I grew to call dad, Eldridge – who along with his wife Marianna adopted me.

Young rising American actor Shane Graham is playing me.

Fucking hell.

It's almost too much to take in.

I really have come full circle.

Most of my earliest memories are of being mistreated or beaten by my biological father.

I hated that bastard.

He's dead now.

I'm having to relive all that pain on set, not only mentally but I'm watching it come to life again – forget magic mushrooms, seeing a film being made about yourself is the most surreal outer body trip you'll ever experience.

In a strange twist, the director and I settled on the decision that I should play my old man, in a nice little cameo.

Maybe no one else could capture what he was like.

We didn't subject cinema-goers to a kid being burned alive, something my father did to me.

In the movie, I just throw the boy close to the fire.

I couldn't stomach recreating it fully.

It's one of the few times I guess when the action on screen isn't a sexed-up version of reality.

If I'm being honest, it was the toughest day of my life, but in some ways the most rewarding.

There was this massive lift when they finally called cut and my time as that asshole was over.

And I'll admit it. As a youngster, I was an asshole too.

I look back in shame at some of the things I did.

Can you believe I was embarrassed by the man who adopted me and, along with his wife, offered me a way out?

And here's the worst part.

I was ashamed of his skin colour.

I didn't want anyone to see me with a black guy.

I was being given a second chance.

So many others never get that.

And here was I, about to almost fuck it up because of all the baggage I was carrying – even as a kid.

I'd been taught to be racist.

If it wasn't for Eldridge and Marianna's love, God knows where I'd be.

I'd never forget the day they took me to see *ET* back in 1982.

Steven Spielberg's epic had me transfixed, sitting there in that cinema in Glasgow.

It was that scene where the group on their bikes flee the police with *ET* – I hadn't a clue what a BMX was.

Coming from where I did, it was never on my radar.

But I was transfixed.

Something inside screamed, 'this is for me'.

I craved the freedom this little two-wheeled contraption offered.

I was a maniac on the bike.

I'd take on all sorts of jumps and stunts.

Let's put it this way, I've broken my skull alone four times, and had more concussions than you've had hot dinners.

But it wasn't having a screw loose that was driving me.

It was the pain and negativity from my old life.

Now I'm older, I realise riding my BMX was mediation.

I was healing my wounds and directing all that rage into a positive outlet.

I was good.

But not as natural as the movie portrays – that's where the screenwriter had a bit of artistic licence.

I wouldn't call myself a gifted rider.

I wasn't born with supreme talent.

But I had determination, due to what I've been through and I'll never take no for an answer – that's why I made it.

And for me, making it wasn't about money or fame.

It was about happiness.

And being able to say, I did it.

That moment came for me when I got the call.

Asking me to become the global brand manager for Haro Bikes.

A lot of the general public might not know Bob Haro.

But he's the godfather and architect of modern BMX riding.

He was also the main stuntman in *ET*.

Now, here I was being handed the baton.

Bob was the face of BMX.

Now, it's me.

Distributing to 80 countries.

I sit down regularly with serious big hitters.

There are billionaires looking to be part of the sport or sign a deal.

And then, there's wee Scottish John at the other side of the table – none of them have a clue about where I've come from and how my life began.

At Haro we have the biggest budget in the sport to give to the pro riders who I feel deserve it.

Most are far more gifted than I ever was.

In the past few years, my athletes have won gold medals at the X Games and represented their countries in the Olympics.

They're the best riders in the world.

I'm essentially their boss.

But I don't see it that way.

I look at it like we're all Team Haro.

And that allows me to make these young riders' dreams come true.

I'm now in control of the BMX company that changed my own life.

I'm now the face of the most famous BMX brand on the planet.

All I've ever had was my passion – and my balls.

Now they've taken me to the top of my sport.

And it's meant Hollywood called and put my life up on the big screen.

I can't believe I've come this far and ended up at a destination so far away and removed from my origins.

I'm living the dream, after living a nightmare.

Like I said, what a ride.

# 1

# Into The Fire

BURNT flesh. That's my first memory. Not exactly the normal thing a person remembers from their childhood, and even worse, it was my own.

I began life with my parents – Thomas and Margaret – in Whiteinch. It's an area in Glasgow, north of the city's River Clyde, which became a busy hub for shipbuilding during the British Empire's heyday. Whiteinch itself grew after it became a popular ferry crossing point.

Back then I was John Craig. That's the name I was given when I was born on 16 March 1972 and it'll become pretty clear why it changed – but let's put it this way, if I'd stayed John Craig, I wouldn't be alive now to write this book.

Glasgow was going through a tumultuous time and a massive transformation was under way to help rescue thousands of families by setting them up in new housing schemes – all outside the city centre.

They were being shipped out of the old tenement buildings, as the level of deprivation was off the charts with no indoor toilets, a lack of hot water and homes were basically riddled with squalor and unhygienic living conditions.

There was also a famous bin strike in 1975, which saw rubbish piled high, and the rats got so comfortable that the city faced an infestation of the buggers. It got so bad that eventually the army was called in to help resolve the situation.

And we were right in the middle of all that, living in one of these same tenements in what's known locally as a room and kitchen – two rooms and a toilet. Even calling one of them a kitchen is a stretch, but it did have a sink. At the back of that was a double bed where we all slept huddled together, apart from my dad, who slept in the other room, on his own a lot of the time. So that was our home. We did have pets though, well if you can count the mice that scurried about the place as that.

To be frank, it was a dump and wasn't much more than a lair for my psycho dad to rule with his violence and bad temper. I think back to living there and what stands out is that it seemed to always be dark and cold. There were no creature comforts. Nothing to think back on and smile about.

I was the third child to arrive and I was only there for the first three years of my life. My older brother Thomas later told me that he started breaking into bakeries to bring some food home as quite often our cupboards were bare. It was seriously grim. And my only real memory is a horrific one. For a long time I actually wondered if it was a dream. Well, a nightmare would be more appropriate.

But my mother told me in later life that it really did happen. Even now I think back and sometimes say, 'Surely it didn't happen like I remember.' But it did.

It happened when I, naive like only a young child can be, was excited to see my dad come home from work – he was a box maker at the shipbuilding firm Yarrow, which manufactured frigates and destroyers for the Royal Navy. Anyway, how was I to know that he'd drunk himself daft on the way back?

He was slouched into the chair in our lounge. It was the sort of chair that screamed 1970s. It had that retro mustard felt and those long, narrow wooden arms. If you watch the TV show *Mad Men*, you'll see something similar.

So he's sitting there, thinking about God knows what, and I decide to run over. I had barely got my arms around his neck when he saw red. Whether I had startled him or woke him up, I don't know. I was three for Christ's sake. But he wanted to make sure I didn't do it again.

He reached over his head, grabbed me around the arms and then hurled me back like a sack of potatoes. I was so small that I flew through the air but as if that wasn't enough, he had thrown me right in the direction of our two-bar electric fire – which was battling in vain to remove the permanent cold chill of our home. They don't exist anymore but it was one of the big iron fireplaces, where the bars light up and glow red with heat. And normally you'd have a grille to stop the chance of anyone getting burned or things catching fire.

Of course, ours didn't. My dad had probably spent the money on booze rather than buy an essential like that. When you've got three kids running around it was hardly something you'd do without. But that was the mark of the man and as I flew through the air, I smacked into the fire. My right foot somehow wedged itself between the bars and was dangling on the red-hot element.

So picture it. I'm lying there, sprawled across the lounge floor. My foot is melting and my dad is still sitting in his chair. The skin was burning off as my sock was melting into my foot. I don't remember the pain but I do remember the smell of my burning flesh. God knows what it would have been like. I'm a father myself now and I can't think of anything worse than seeing my kids suffer like that. But he sat there.

My mother rushed in and prised my foot out of the fire. I can't recall properly but our next door neighbour was a nurse or some sort of paramedic; I just remember they were called in as they had some medical skills. But they took one look and told my mum, 'John has to go to hospital immediately.' We didn't have a car so my poor mum scooped me up and rushed down the stairs in our block. We were going by public bus.

I was being carried along the night-time streets as my mangled foot was still hissing and sizzling away. Clear watery liquid was seeping out of my foot and the puss was dripping off my toes.

And as if that wasn't enough, it was also smack bang in the middle of what became known as the Winter of Discontent and the bin strike was in full swing. But bigger than that, it was a time of massive upheaval as the miners had also taken industrial action and the country was suffering from electrical blackouts due to the lack of coal. So my mother was dodging the mounds of rubbish on the dark streets as the lights were out.

I think the pain heightened my other senses and I was overcome by the stench. As my mum ran through it, avoiding the army of rats, it was like breathing in dog shit all the way to the hospital. You couldn't escape it – and instead of being tucked up in my bed or having a game of dominos like the other three-year-olds, I was out in it.

Finally we got there. I must have passed out. My mother told me when I was an adult and I could stomach it that the staff were actually peeling off my sock with my skin. It had all become one big melted mess. I was so badly burned that they then had to do a skin graft, so a chunk was shaved off my ass and then transferred on to my foot. It healed pretty well and there's only a small amount of scarring left today. But I was left with an odd birth mark on my foot, which is the exact same size and shape as the birth mark on my backside.

So that's all my father gave me in this world. A weird birth mark that's split between my ass and my right foot – thanks for nothing ya prick.

* * * * *

After quite literally going from the frying pan into the fire, I got out of hospital and the Craig family moved. Following my horrendous time you would imagine that it could only get better. Surely the new place would be happier and give me, and us all, the chance of a new start. Sadly, no.

Our time at 18 Glenkirk Drive was even more traumatic. I didn't know it then but it was to be the last place I'd live with my parents. It wasn't much of a step up but at least it was a 'four' apartment – there were three bedrooms and a living room. But you'd still call it a dump.

It wasn't too far away but we were now in Drumchapel, known locally as The Drum. It's one of the famed housing estates where Glasgow's working-class families were dropped into. Sadly it didn't prosper as gangs took over and it was a cut-throat environment – not somewhere you'd ideally want to raise a young family.

The one highlight for me was it was brighter than our first home at least. We were up in the top left apartment. And soon after we arrived my mum fell pregnant with my younger sister Agnes, but she nearly never made it as my pathetic dad became even more vicious. Even his biggest supporter could argue that he didn't plan to melt my foot but what he did to my mother was totally intentional.

As usual he was pissed. He stormed in from work and my mother was in the kitchen making him his dinner. She had chips – a Glasgow staple – on the go but the fucking clown wasn't having it. He wasn't prepared to wait so he marched into the kitchen, grabbed the boiling hot frying pan and splashed some of the bubbling oil across her face. Then he used the leverage of the steel pan to snap her arm like a twig.

As the poor woman was left as a crumpled mess on the floor, he turned around and snarled, 'Make sure my fucking dinner is ready next time I get home, bitch.'

That was our home. I had my own beating in that kitchen, that I endured after being caught stealing some biscuits.

I was about five. I'd dragged myself up on to the counter and I was looking to chow down a cheeky snack. Now, we were poor so there were no fancy chocolate chip cookies or anything like that. It was fucking dry tea biscuits, that's all our coffers stretched to. But as a kid I didn't know any different and they were a serious treat in my eyes.

Just as my fingers reached the tin and began dragging it across the shelf, in walked my pathetic excuse for a father. Incensed by catching me – I don't know if he felt I was challenging his authority or if he just enjoyed hurting others – he got me by the scruff of the neck and launched me backwards, slamming into the opposite wall. I helplessly slid down to the floor. He'd winded me badly and left me lying there like a wet bath towel.

Another nice addition my old man made to me is the scar I have on the back right of my head. I'd been out the back at the bins again. I was what is known in Glasgow as a 'midgie raker', basically a dirty wee bastard who was into everything and played around in the bins. I fancied a glass of milk so instead of coming up via the stairs I shinned up the drainpipe and got to our kitchen window. It was three floors up so I was fairly high – and it had a big set of windows that slid sideways, but the smaller top pane opened outwards.

It was open and I hauled myself in. Either my dad heard me or happened to come into the kitchen, just as I was half in, half out. He smacked me on the back of the head with a thick walking stick, opening up a gash on the back of my napper. And the force meant I came crashing down into the sink, banging my face on the taps and basin. I was like a yelping puppy, leaping out of the sink and crawling away through his legs out of the door to safety. The pain was unreal and I still have the scar today to prove it.

That was what our house was like on a daily basis but my brother actually got it worse than me. Not only had he been around longer, he was bigger of course so my dad must have thought he could take more punishment. But

Thomas started hanging out with a gang and was getting himself into trouble, causing mischief in the area.

I was too young for that so I started just not going home. Sometimes I would jump on the train into Glasgow city centre to beg for money and occasionally I'd sleep on the streets. I'd wander around, basically just killing time so I didn't have to be at home. Any minute not spent there was a positive for me.

I had to scavenge food to satisfy my hunger pangs – I was a growing boy after all. So I'd live up to my nickname and rake through the bins at the Chinese takeaway near our house. I remember eating some of the leftovers and looking over to see a dead dog's carcass being devoured by maggots. Even to this day, when I walk past a bin that rancid smell hits my tongue and causes me to gag.

That isn't something a five-year-old boy should be experiencing, although I did at least get to indulge my biscuit cravings when one of the shops had thrown out custard creams in the same bins. I'd never had them in my life. These were the upmarket things we never had in our cupboards. I was so naive and I wolfed them down. But they were actually covered in mould – that's why they were chucked away. Plus they'd been lying in the bin. They tasted fucking horrible. But what choice did I have?

I don't even remember having any wee mates or going out to play. My only friend was Graham Hughes, who lived downstairs. He seemed to get a hard time off his dad but I don't think it was up there with my living hell. I think in some way that made us more comrades forced together rather than big pals. We used to play fighters around the back of our flats, knocking seven bells of shit out of each other – both hands and feet were allowed, it was serious stuff and blood was spilled. I must have been an able sparring partner as Graham went on to become a decent amateur boxer at lightweight.

We also developed a fascination for the flat on the bottom opposite Graham's place as we were convinced it was haunted. I recall looking through the letterbox and seeing the hand from *The Addams Family* running around in there. So that was my recreation, aside from keeping myself safe and fed, by hook or by crook.

But if you thought I had it bad, my poor mum was sharing a bed with this demon of a husband. If you're wondering why I had so much time to do my own thing it was because my mother was petrified of him too. She didn't want to be at home either. Any excuse and she tried to get out. I had butterflies every time she left as I didn't want her to go. In some ways, she was my safety net.

I felt better and more comfortable when she was there – like I had someone who wanted to protect me. But I don't blame her. How can I?

Looking back now, what kind of life was it experiencing the horror of seeing your sons slapped around and being used yourself as a punchbag? Due to my mum being absent, I somehow got in tow with a local girl, Yvonne Musley, who was double my age.

She was the first girl I kissed and we sort of ended up with a twisted younger brother/older sister thing, with benefits. Until I was a lot older, she was the only female I was able to relax around.

Even when my mum was there, I was on tenterhooks that she was about to flee – so I was never relaxed. I paid the ultimate tribute to Yvonne by using a match and burning the skin off my arm to tattoo her name – but I thought it was spelt Evon.

I'm sad to say that Yvonne died in a car accident 20 years ago and from all accounts didn't have the best of lives. I hope that was nothing to do with me, but it shows that the part of the world we were coming from was no easy ride.

That was also highlighted by my own auntie Evy – my dad's sister – and her boyfriend Ian Adams, when they callously chopped up their neighbour. The story went that Ian owed the guy downstairs some money and when he came up to ask for it back Ian murdered him. They both then gruesomely chopped up the poor guy's body. First they tried to burn him in the coal fire but that didn't work, so they stuffed the severed limbs and torso in black bags and threw them in a wardrobe. The smell got so bad that eventually people called the authorities and Ian ended up getting a hefty prison sentence.

That was the type of thing we lived with and in among. My mum's family cut us off totally as because of my dad they didn't want to know, and you can understand why.

Part of my mum's coping strategy was that she would spend time at the house of another guy in the area, but she'd always come home at night. I don't know if they were having an affair or if it was just her getting shelter. Maybe that was one of the reasons for my dad's even more volatile behaviour. But that's no excuse.

I could never make a case for that bastard. I can't believe my ears when my sister Rachel does. She does it to this day. I've heard her say things like, 'he wasn't that bad'.

What the fuck. Maybe it's because he didn't beat her as due to some fucked-up moral code, he didn't hit my sisters. It wasn't a woman thing as my mum was regularly knocked about.

Maybe my sister is in denial or it could be her way of dealing with it. I've told her straight, 'What fucking planet are you on? He almost murdered our mother and destroyed our family.'

And he even caused me to end my own part in it forever, on Christmas Eve 1979.

\* \* \* \* \*

Christmas is normally a time full of happy, joyous memories. Sitting around the tree, opening presents, pulling crackers and telling the awful jokes inside them to the rest of the family – or watching your dad carve up the turkey before everyone tucks in; Christmas songs blasting out.

But not in the Craig household. The first Christmas I remember is harrowing. The clock had just turned over into Christmas Eve in 1979 and God knows why I was still up after midnight as a seven-year-old, but I was.

I don't know how, but I was aware of a commotion between my mother and father. I think my developing virgin brain purposely didn't retain every detail, for its own sake. I went into the room and there was my old man, pinning her to the bed. His left hand was wedged across her throat, keeping her from getting up. And his right hand was chopping back and forth, smashing into her face. It was like a mechanical piston in a car engine, just firing up and down. I remember seeing it almost in isolation, as if I couldn't see anything else apart from his arm.

Then my brain went into self-preservation mode again. No young child should be arming themselves with a blade, but I did. I must have gotten it from the kitchen. My memory kicks back in at this point.

As I charged at my dad, my plan was to stab him in the abdomen, to ram that knife right into his vital organs and get my mother to safety somehow – but I was seven. He saw me coming out the corner of his eye and as I came racing across the room, he turned around and smash. That's when it goes black.

I was told in later life by my mother than he knocked me out cold. I'm pretty sure I was concussed as I don't remember a damn thing, from surging at him brandishing the blade until the next lunchtime.

Somehow I was woken up, dressed and packed off to school for the final day before the Christmas holidays.

My memory cuts back in here as maybe the daze from being socked by my dad had worn off – and I'm in the lunch hall. We'd been served up a festive treat of sponge cake with custard. Bloody delicious. And in my house, it wasn't something we got laid down in front of us.

So I was lapping it up, happy as Larry, proving just how dysfunctional a family we were. There I was, sitting without a care in the world, devouring my pudding – literally 12 hours after I'd tried to knife my own father while he brutally attacked my mother. Jesus Christ.

As I cheerily licked my bowl clean, I was summoned to the headmistress's office. I swaggered in; that's how I walked in those days – I was a hard man, or so I thought anyway. Waiting for me there was a social worker and a policeman. I didn't know at the time but they were all aware of the previous night's high jinks.

After some chit-chat, I was bundled into the cop car and we drove away. We stopped to collect my sister Agnes from nursery as she was only two at the time. And that was it. I never, ever went back to 18 Glenkirk Drive and I never, ever lived with my parents again. The Craig family was no more. Over in the blink of an eye.

But because of the immediacy of the situation, there was nowhere for us to go. We hung about at the social work department for hours. We didn't realise, but they were obviously scrambling about, trying to put a roof over our heads. Then at 10.30pm, we were driven across a dark and dreary Glasgow. Most kids our age were putting out the milk and cookies for Santa, hanging up their stockings and struggling to sleep due to all the excitement. We weren't.

We were being checked into Glenrosa Children's Home, which was a detached villa that had been converted. It's not there anymore as it was shut down by the city after years of complaints from nearby residents of unruly kids involved in violent and booze-related incidents. And even in my day, it was as far from a cosy and cheery family house as you could get. But it was certainly a lot better than what I'd left.

It was where kids who had problems or no one to look after them ended up. I ended up in a cell with three other lads. It was grim. But it was by far and away the best Christmas present I've ever been given. And who gave it to me? My own mother.

She was the one who had tipped off the police about the knife incident. I only found out as an adult that she bravely did that, knowing full well they would take her kids off her and knowing my dad would have killed me. And not in the metaphorical sense – literally. He was the sort of character who was capable of it.

And with me standing up to him, it was only a matter of time. He couldn't have dealt with his son standing up to him and the next time he got home drunk, I was sure to be on the hit-list. I didn't know it then but my mum saved my life – sacrificing being with us, to get us to a safer place. And while it was a still a long way back to normality and having a future, it was the first step – and I thank my lucky stars every single day I got to take it.

The staff at Glenrosa even did their bit to welcome us. I was furnished with two gifts from the home. They would have told me they were from Santa – and that the big fella obviously got the call late on, but still knew where to leave my presents. The thing was, I didn't believe in Santa. It was never mentioned in the Craig household and we didn't get presents. So as well as a new home, I was ripping open wrapping paper for the first time.

Maybe in the rush, the elves got my name mixed up – it's understandable. I was given a Buck Rogers gun but on the tag, it had David scored out and John written beneath. It's an easy mistake to make, they both sound alike! I never did find out who David was or what happened to him, but if you're reading this – I'll buy you a beer any time if we're ever in the same place as compensation.

The other thing I was given was a panda teddy bear, wearing a red and white polkadot waistcoat. You might think that a hardened wee guy who was capable of stabbing his dad would have been embarrassed by such a soppy present. But, no. I adored that teddy and it was in my bed every single night I spent in Glenrosa until I left. And if you manage to see the movie that's been made of my life you'll see it in there too, although the producers swapped it for a dog. Maybe that's a bit cooler.

But I didn't give a shit. I loved my panda, although I would never had admitted it. It became like my comfort blanket.

Although that wasn't the only thing going on under the sheets in Glenrosa.

# 2

# Thug Life

LOOK, I'll lay my cards on the table. I bloody loved Glenrosa. Most people I talk to are expecting me to say that I hated it. It was like prison. Exactly like you see on TV. It was a jungle, dog eat dog.

At the start, I did end up in scraps as I was handy with my fists. And from my background, you didn't back down – neither did the rest of the boys in there, and it didn't take much for things to go off like a Molotov cocktail. But things quickly calmed down for me as the law of the jungle soon kicked in. I realised that everyone had their pack and I found mine too.

After that settling in was pretty easy. We had the convict's mentality – we were institutionalised. Everything was scheduled; we didn't have to make any decisions, nor did we have any freedom.

There was no education going on in there so we'd be transported to the nearby primary school. I struggled terribly and couldn't read or write, as my romantic tattoo experiments had proven. But I never felt embarrassed or ashamed. None of the other pupils said anything to the Glenrosa squad. Why not?

Pretty simple. We'd smash their fucking faces in – and then go to work on their bodies, if need be. That became clear after a few teething incidents. They were naive and didn't realise where we were coming from. The sight of blood didn't faze us, it spurred us on. We had all been through so much that violence had become normality, and in lots of ways we were old beyond our years.

Glenrosa gave me a sense of belonging. I had my pack. It was a brotherhood, and that was reinforced even more when we'd go to school. We'll roll in like a platoon, do the job and then roll out, so I adapted very quickly. I liked being in there and even better, I was away from my father. He was no longer around to scare or beat me. But it wasn't a model existence.

There was a poor boy in there who suffered from mental issues. None us of knew what and to be frank, none of us gave a shit – none of us had the skills to empathise or worry about what he was going through. If you weren't of use to us, then you'd get used by us. And we'd rip him to shreds, do all sorts to drive him wild. Annoy him. Badger him. You name it, we did it – we were sick bastards. We really were twisted as it'd always end up the same way. He'd have this kind of fit, when something in him just couldn't handle the pressure and he would snap like a twig. Next thing, he'd lash out at us and get stuck in and he'd kick all our asses, no bother. This guy was as strong as an ox and had the power of a bloody Panzer tank. But to think back and see myself tormenting someone with mental issues, just so I could laugh at them – that makes me fucking ashamed. I could never do that now but I relished it back then.

And another thing I revelled in was the late-night handjobs. We had this rather tasty-looking night nurse, who must have been in her late teens or early 20s and must have applied for the job as she seemed to like younger men. Well, ten-year-olds to be frank.

So quite often at night, she'd go around our cell tucking all four of us in but then the hand would slip down under the sheets and she'd wank us off. I would lie there thinking, 'I'm the fucking man.' I'm a father myself now and if anyone did that to my kid I would fucking throttle them and take the consequences of ending up in the electric chair if need be – I'm that serious. It was totally out of order and should not have been happening, but that was Glenrosa. Violence. Pack mentality. Law of the jungle. And cheeky handjobs. What was not to like?

And while I was relishing life in Glenrosa, I never thought back to what was happening at home – it really never crossed my mind. I was just glad to be out of that hellhole. But in later life my mother did confide in me about what it was like, as apparently my dad was incandescent.

By the time Agnes and I were taken away and put into care, my brother Thomas had been sent to the juvenile detention unit Oakbank in Aberdeen, up in the north-east of Scotland. It was a borstal for young delinquents, as he'd been stealing, not going to school and getting into plenty of trouble. My older sister Rachel was in another unit too, as she'd been skipping school and the authorities had stepped in to deal with her. So every one of my siblings was no longer in the flat and my father blamed my mother. What a selfish prick. I don't think he could process that it was he who had caused us all to end up in these different institutions. It was hardly a coincidence that the Craig kids had a perfect 100 per cent record of being admitted and removed from the home.

Or maybe he knew it was him and just didn't want to admit it. I can only imagine the pain my poor mother was in. She told me later in life how he flew into a rage every so often and would shout at her for losing all their kids. Of course, there was more violence.

I wasn't around and she never told me the details, but I can only think about what it was like for her. There were no kids for her to love. Nothing to give her that ray of happiness among the complete shit situation she was in. It was just her – and that beast.

I did see her though and I'd still get those butterflies. The school I would be bused to and from Glenrosa every day had a big red ash pitch. For those outside of Scotland, it's a football park but without grass and made up of ground-up tiny stones, all compacted together. And the colour is this deep reddy-brown – hence that name. Due to the surface, any form of ball games on them resulted in scraped knees and severely ripped school trousers or skirts. Parents must have hated them, but they required no maintenance and that's why most schools had one.

Anyway, during break and lunchtime, we'd be out on it. I wasn't a big footballer but I'd be hanging out with my brotherhood. And around the school's perimeter was this wire fence – it stopped any balls spilling out on to the road and causing a car crash.

Every so often I'd spy my mother standing there. She was not supposed to be doing that – any visit to see Agnes and me was supposed to be handled under strict supervision, through the proper channels. But she'd disregard that and come down, and no wonder, imagine having all your kids taken away. You'd couldn't help but go down and see them if they were that close by. And that's what she did.

I'd trot over and we didn't have long or meaningful chats. To me all this sort of upheaval and trauma was pretty normal. I would still get those butterflies though, as I wanted her love. I wanted her attention and to a greater degree, her affection. Subconsciously I craved to have my mother.

She would force packets of pickled onion crisps and Yorkie chocolate bars through the fence as both were my favourites. I never told anyone about her secret visits as they were something for us to share. But she would obviously go when lessons began so again I was used to her leaving me for whatever reason.

Needless to say, my dad never showed up. When I was admitted to Glenrosa, I only saw him twice again until he died in 1997.

One of those visits was when he came to Glenrosa in 1981. There's a photograph of it and as they say, a picture is worth a thousand words. In this case, that's probably true as if you just took it at face value, we look a pretty happy father and son. But if you look really closely, you can see my dad looks a bit fragile because he'd suffered a massive stroke.

Ironically it happened on the day that he'd been paid off by Yarrows. As he finished his final shift, he collapsed on the premises just as he was walking out. It was a serious one. They rushed him to hospital and from what I was told, they did all they could for him. But he was left a shadow of himself and was completely paralysed all down his left side. They kept him in for about three months and my brother – who was now back – told me later in life, that he never went to visit him once, he was hoping he'd never get out.

I was glad to hear that when he got home, his violence and rage was all gone. Thomas said it stopped not because my dad had seen the error of his ways – he simply wasn't physically able to knock them about anymore.

And when I saw him that day in Glenrosa, he definitely wasn't the same person I'd been terrorised by. He had this sort of daft grin on his face a lot of the time.

Did I feel sorry for him? No fucking way. He'd put me through hell and I had no sympathy for that bastard whatsoever and it was going to be a long time before I really forgave both my parents for what went on.

\* \* \* \* \*

Life kept on going at Glenrosa and like I've said, I had my wee gang. I was in my groove, I felt good and comfortable in my environment. And better still, I knew how things operated and had a routine. But then in 1982, it was time for things to change – and it wasn't going to be my choice.

Eldridge and Marianna Buultjens were a pair of academics. Eldridge was born in Sri Lanka but came over to Britain to further his education and he had become a research scientist at the University of Glasgow by this point – plus he'd also got a PhD in some sort of complicated biology, which is way past my pay grade. His wife worked at Kelvin School, which was for blind children. They didn't have any of their own offspring and wanted to adopt more than one kid – and applied through the children's charity Barnardo's. Whatever selection process they went through, they were matched with Agnes and me.

The social workers told them about us and my new parents to be were keen on us as they wanted to keep us together as a family. I do feel they got the short end of the stick with me, this violent ten-year-old boy. It's like signing up to buy a new car and the salesman says you have to take a rusty old caravan that's infested with bats as part of the deal. Amazingly, Eldridge and Marianna agreed and followed through on their commitment of wanting to keep a broken family together. That showed the mark of them and makes my initial thoughts about them even more cringeworthy.

The first time I was introduced to them and given some of the detail about maybe living with them down the line, I was furious. The words in my mind were, 'What the fuck?' I said that there was no way I was living with any black man. I had never come across any black people before and I'd been raised in a culture where racist comments were not only acceptable, but encouraged.

I saw nothing wrong with looking down on someone because of their colour and thinking my white skin was superior. Black people to me weren't on my level, they were beneath me and certainly weren't to be respected. Imagine facing that from a wee boy.

But still, Eldridge wasn't put off. It can't have been easy for Marianna to have her husband made to feel that way either. Both Agnes and I were given a scrapbook, which I've still got today, titled 'An Introduction to Eldridge and Marianna'. It was about their lives, what they were like and how they spent their days. It also introduced us to the other key member of the family,

Molly the cat – who I must say, ruled the roost in that house. The book had printed across its cover 'To John and Agnes' and it really was lovely, but at the time I was still bitter and felt my little bubble was about to burst. So I was against it.

I didn't want to go and dug my heels in. I wanted to stay in the children's home that was full of other dysfunctional kids like me. I reckon I was just scared of change and was so used to battling through life, that I didn't want to contemplate giving up control. But the social workers pressed on and a day trip was arranged so Eldridge and Marianna picked us up.

I remember it like it was yesterday, as it was my first time in a car that didn't belong to the police or the social work department. The four of us loaded into their canary yellow Nissan and off we went. To me it was a limousine, it was a serious bit of kit – coming from the place I had, where a mouldy biscuit was seen as a luxury. And while I was very impressed to be in such a nice motor, there was no way in hell I was going to let them know that.

I'd never been to the West End of Glasgow. It has always been, and still is, the most affluent part of the city. It plays host to fancy delicatessens, cheese shops, vintage clothing stores and bespoke jewellery makers. Another world from my days in Whiteinch with the rotting dead dog being ravaged by maggots outside the dingy Chinese takeaway.

We pulled up at their flat at 47 Kelvinside Gardens. It was one of the old-style stone buildings; high ceilings, big bay windows, it was a palace. The major thoughts in my head were, 'These two are fucking loaded, they're rich and how the hell did this black guy get so much money?'

We had a few more visits then within a few months, we spent the weekend there. Progress was quite quick and a month down the line we were moving in full-time. I was still against it, even on that first day when we made the big move. I was standing in this massive bedroom, the same size as the cell back in Glenrosa, but I had shared that with three other lads. This was all for me.

Eldridge and Marianna had shelled out on kitting it all out. I had a bed, a desk – which was ironic considering I couldn't really write and could barely read. Everything was brand new. There were nice polished floorboards, with an area rug over them. It was the Taj Mahal compared to what I'd been used to and there I was still thinking, 'I want to get the fuck out of here.' Because of that, I did my level best to mess it up.

For the first six months with Eldridge and Marianna, I was like the Tasmanian devil. I was out of control. I was a terror and they must have wondered why on earth they agreed to take me on. But they never showed it. They were patient and kept trying to get through to me.

Meanwhile, I did my level best to drive them up the wall. I didn't fit in such a well-to-do area which was at odds with what I felt comfortable in, and maybe I was insecure and acted up to hide it. I was picking fights and more than once I was brought back by the police. Eldridge and Marianna had never dealt with the boys in blue, for God's sake.

The worst time was when one of my wee pals and I decided to leave our homes for good. We started walking and flagged down a car and neither of us really knew what we were doing but the family inside were going to Irvine so we jumped in. During the ride, they must have smelled a rat and thankfully they were salt-of-the-earth folk so they promptly dropped us at the police station when we arrived.

My parents had to drive down to pick me up – it's a good 45 minutes by car – so it must have been a pretty big shock for them. They couldn't have showed how much they loved me any more clearly, literally coming down to bring me back to a wonderful home they'd provided for me.

So in some ways, I was still living by the values I'd picked up from my earlier days. Violence and racism was my mantra. I'd been enrolled at Dunard Primary School, which wasn't far away at all. In fact, thanks to the wonders of Google Maps, I can now see that it was precisely a seven-minute walk. But my route took me past Saint Charles' Primary School, which was a Catholic school and mine wasn't. So of course there was the usual rivalry by some loudmouths when they spotted wee John walking by in a different uniform. But what they didn't know was what I was capable of.

They were from this nice affluent area so hadn't been through some of the life lessons that I had – and one I had learned, was to fight my corner.

I remember a group of five boys came out, intent on giving me a hard time as I was on their patch. They were led by a pair of burly brothers who were known in the local area as Mick 'The Prick' and Frank 'The Wank'. Not the most inventive names, but they did the job in the playground. They and their cronies had me surrounded but the thing was, coming from where I did, in that situation you just fought fire with fire. So I gave the biggest of them – I think it was Frank – a Glasgow Kiss.

For anyone who doesn't know, that's basically a headbutt but you drive your skull forcefully forward and look to crack their nose open right on the bridge. It's an art, not easy to carry out. Well, I delivered mine that day to perfection, the guy's knees buckled with the impact and down he went. I dropped him on the pavement. The other four backed off as they didn't want to end up there too and that was the last time anyone from Saint Charles' gave me grief on my daily commute.

The law of the jungle was still my code of ethics.

# 3

# Decision Time

WHILE I was still not enamoured to be living with Eldridge and Marianna, things were going well at school – socially, that is. My violent tendencies meant that any problems were quickly resolved. The kids in that area hadn't seen what I'd seen and I can now say as a grown man, I'm glad they hadn't. But they didn't have that edge that I did. So I was able to slot in and not have any problems.

My academic performance was horrendous as I couldn't read or write properly. I spoke in a lot of slang, plus I had serious issues pronouncing things properly, as I was tongue tied. So if I wanted to say lorry, it came out sounding like lolly – I finally got that corrected after getting the ligament snipped off.

But grades didn't feature on my radar. I didn't give a shit as things at home weren't quite to my liking. It was probably me just looking to not fit in rather than any real problems. I couldn't or wouldn't adjust to Eldridge and Marianna's way of doing things. If something didn't please them or they felt they had to give me some guidance, they did it verbally. I was perplexed by this. There were no beatings or physical confrontations, they wanted to talk. There was no getting hurt or wounds to tend. I was like a feral animal and not domesticated to live like that.

My own insecurities made me react badly to their more sophisticated ways and due to my immaturity, instead of admitting to myself that I had to adjust, I just threw my toys out of the pram. I was struggling. One way of coping was to steal from them. To me, Eldridge and Marianna were rich beyond belief when in reality, they were well off and comfortable but by no means wealthy.

I didn't get this then. I'd never been around a middle-class way of life, so not having to scrape by from meal to meal meant you were loaded to me. I remember going with Eldridge for my first visit to an ATM. Well, I say with. The embarrassment of living with a black man was enough but I definitely didn't want to be seen with him in public. I didn't want my great reputation to be sullied by being caught in the company of a non-white.

So as we went down Great Western Road, a bustling main street in our area, I was about five metres behind. It was enough for him not to keep stopping for me but far enough so anyone going by on a bus wouldn't think that John Craig hung around with darkies. I did get close enough to see this crisp money being dispensed. I was stunned. Fucking hell, you can get cash out of the wall? I remember making a mental note, thinking 'I'll be having some of that, mate' – and I did.

I would go into Eldridge's wallet or Marianna's bag and steal, taking a £10 or £20 note at a time. Then I'd splash the cash on the way to school like I was Al Capone. It was a lot of dosh for a ten-year-old to have, when Atari games were only five pence, so I was living it up and didn't give a shit about stabbing Eldridge and Marianna in the back.

But then at school my big mouth of a girlfriend, Sharon Bisset, told the headmistress. You'd think she'd know the role of a gangster's moll is to keep her trap shut. We were kissing and all sorts, so to me I had her undying loyalty but she blabbed and my criminal empire came crashing down. The worst part of it all was when Eldridge said to the headmistress, 'We already knew about it, it's okay.'

Instead of feeling ashamed, I was more bemused. If I thought someone was stealing from me I'd have got tooled up and gone to work on them, given them a black eye and a few sore ribs at the very least. Plus I also felt inferior as I had myself down as street smart and here was this boring academic making me look bad, by saying he knew about my scam all along.

So I stopped doing it, but I think their way of dealing with it and accepting things meant there was always going to be an issue assimilating a child like me into their house – and that rankled with me. It started to hit home that I wasn't in control and it all really kicked off one night at dinner time.

We were having sprouts and I was either not eating them or I didn't want them. Eldridge was trying to talk to me and say 'you need to eat your vegetables', like any responsible father would.

But I couldn't handle this way of acting so I flipped out and began smashing my head off the ceramic tiles on the kitchen floor. I was rattling my traumatised brain to try and sort out the confusion going on in there. I was like a robot that had short-circuited. I just couldn't settle and I wasn't shy to let Eldridge and Marianna know that.

It came to a head about six months in when I demanded that our social worker Colin Turban was called. I wanted him summoned and told him that I wasn't living with these people anymore, I wanted to be taken back and readmitted to Glenrosa immediately. So being the big-hearted people they are, Eldridge and Marianna did exactly that. Colin turned up and I told him, 'Take me back.'

He didn't put up a fight or try to talk me out of it. My stuff was packed up into bags, which didn't take long as practically everything in my room belonged to Eldridge and Marianna anyway. We trudged down to the car and just as he slipped the key into the ignition, he turned to me and said, 'John, if you leave here, you'll be dead by the time you're 16.'

It was a pretty big thing to say to a youngster, but I could handle it. He went on to tell me he'd never seen a pair of parents offer so much unconditional love and support. They had not flinched about taking on two kids – and a rowdy boy at that. They had not buckled when faced with my outrageous behaviour and attitude. They had accepted my blatant racism and still wanted me. Colin told me this was my only chance. And that sentence hit me like a lightning bolt.

Something right there and then clicked and I realised it was this, death or prison. The path I was on was so destructive and clearly just going to get worse. I was a car crash waiting to happen and I decided it was time to turn the corner. I told Colin to let me out and I went back into the house. I faced up to Eldridge and Marianna, this couple who had been so fucking nice to me and were offering me a life full of love and opportunities for no reason other than they wanted to help me – and my little sister, of course. I was in floods of tears as it all came pouring out of me. They were crying too. We'd become a family in that instant – the bond was sealed then.

None of us could explain it properly, but it happened. Then I did something I'd never done in my life before – I uttered the word 'sorry'. And I was.

I was so caught up in the emotion that I never even noticed Colin slipping out of the house but my life was about to finally change and take me on a completely different path. I never saw Colin again. So if you're reading this, thank you for what you said to me that day sitting in your car – without it, I wouldn't have done or seen any of the wonderful things I have.

* * * * *

Waking up the next day, I was a different person – it was the beginning of who I am today. The racism and the hunger for violence all began to gradually seep out of me and disappear. Don't get me wrong, it wasn't gone overnight, but it had started to leave. I was becoming part of society and more importantly, part of a family.

As that happened Eldridge and Marianna became my mum and dad in my eyes. From then on, whenever I mentioned my parents I meant them, not the man and woman who brought me into the world.

Eldridge and Marianna are closer to me than blood and it is ridiculous to think I could have thrown it all away. I started to accept that I wasn't in control and instead I began to do my duties around the house. I helped with the washing-up, put my clothes away in the cupboard and I was finally starting to live like a normal kid. We'd go to the park or get the marbles out and have a match.

I started to let my mum and dad in, to open up and give them a part of me. We bonded and I embraced their affection – it was all to do with being accepted for me. In my damaged mind my biological mother had shunned me and got rid of me, like you throw out an old fur coat. I had found an acceptance among my brotherhood in Glenrosa but now I was together as part of a real family with two loving parents and my sister.

One of the normal things that came with this new life was spending time with my dad, bonding – man to man, if you like. I can't recall ever doing anything on my own with my biological father but Eldridge was a completely different kettle of fish and we had stacks of good times. The best has to be when he took the whole family to see *ET* in December 1982. It was the big blockbuster release for the Christmas cinema-goers and everyone was talking about it. If you hadn't gone, then you were seriously out of the loop.

We went to the theatre near our home, The Grosvenor, which is still there today but has been totally refurbished and is actually a pretty trendy place to watch a movie. I stood outside just last year, almost 35 years to the day that we went to see Steven Spielberg's epic and thought back to us all clambering inside.

That day I lapped it up as it was a superb film for a kid, full of emotion, excitement and enlightenment. But the scene when the BMX bikes appeared on screen was what grabbed me. It changed my life forever. I was fascinated by these fantastic machines but before that I had never been interested in bikes, let alone a BMX. I'd never had one and never wanted one. But seeing the alien cowering in the basket under a towel as Elliott cycled along, going like the clappers and jumping off pavements, speeding over hills – while being chased by the police. Whoa!

I was transfixed. Nothing had ever looked cooler or appealed to me more. I came out of that cinema with BMX burned into my brain – even the alien thing had not hit home as hard with me. My mum and dad took us for burgers after it, and they still remember me just sitting there completely star-struck by what I'd seen. But it wasn't because of the big emotional ending, like my sister who was crying her eyes out – mine were as wide as saucers, transfixed by the bikes.

And I was chomping at the bit to get a taste of it myself so I pestered my dad until he took me to a BMX club in Glasgow. It wasn't much but to me it was a theatre of dreams with riders whizzing around this track and going hell for leather. You rented the bikes and used your time wisely so as to get maximum bang for your buck. I gripped the handlebars and I was off. The feeling didn't disappoint. I was charging around there like a bull in a china shop – it was fantastic. We went back again soon after. And again.

But I needed my own machine so once again my mum and dad stepped in and made it happen when they treated me to my very own BMX when I turned 11. And they even let me choose it on 10 March 1983, six days before my official birthday. I was the BMX king of the house after all. I mean, I had extensive knowledge of the sport after three riding sessions and I'd studied the riding skills demonstrated in *ET* intensely!

Basically there were two machines in the running at Dales Cycles in Glasgow, which is still around today. In the red corner we had the flashy all-chrome Piranha XL. It had these eye-catching mag wheels. If you don't know what mag wheels are, they're the ones with big chunky arms inside the wheel that look cool and are very retro now, whereas normal wheels have the metal spokes. And in the blue corner was the challenger, a Diamondback Viper. It was a more elegant-looking bike and that's because it was lighter and designed like a pro's model.

What did I do? Well, being a man who's always wanted to make an impression, I opted for the Piranha. It was completely the wrong choice, mainly because not only were the wheels big but they were made of steel as this was before nylon was being used. So they were bloody heavy and meant my bike wasn't going to be any sort of speed machine. But back then, I didn't give a shit.

I was bursting with pride. It was the first piece of property that was really mine, that had been bought with only me in mind – I was meticulous about keeping it clean, and it's a trait I've still got today with my possessions. I think coming from fuck all hammers that into you. And instead of my mum driving it home for me, I mounted my pride and joy, setting off on the journey myself.

I was hooked by just having the freedom to blast down the pavement with the wind in my hair and a smile on my face. It was freedom. It was enjoyment. It was about me expressing myself. All the things my life had lacked in my earlier years, I was finally experiencing right there on the saddle of my Piranha.

As I pedalled like fury, I could never have imagined that several decades later I would be the face of and the global brand manager for Haro BMX in California. It's the company started by Bob Haro, who was a stunt rider in *ET*. He's the guy wearing the balaclava in the movie's legendary chase scene as the cops pursue the BMXers in their bid to capture the alien. And then Bob went on to create the most prestigious BMX brand in the world – but getting there, like most things in my life, wasn't going to be a straightforward affair.

# 4

# John Buultjens

MY obsession was no flash in the pan but as this was still the early 1980s, BMX wasn't the global phenomenon that it was set to become. There were few magazines or TV programmes kicking about. I didn't have them on my radar anyway – I was only really living out my BMX in my head, I hadn't connected to any other part of the sport. Part of that might have been my neck of the woods in Glasgow, which as I've mentioned before was pretty affluent. You needed a few quid to have a nice place there – and my parents did.

Now that I had finally accepted them and stopped being such a wee prick, I was becoming domesticated. I had never done dishes. I had never set a table. I had never tidied things up behind me. But I'd started to do all that, slowly at first but I got going and became receptive to lending a hand around the house.

So I was feeling enjoyment from being part of a family, mucking in, taking on tasks. The thing I found hardest to adjust to, and it wasn't until later in life that the penny dropped, was that living in a clean household wasn't natural for me. I always felt I didn't belong. There was something about it, maybe I didn't feel I deserved to be in that sort of environment. I was a wee grubby bastard and I was insecure – I felt if something was too good or nice it wasn't real or wasn't going to last, but I began to feel more and more comfortable thanks to my parents.

The biggest culture shock was potpourri. When I first clapped eyes on a bowl of it, I was like, 'What the fuck is that?' I didn't know it you were supposed to eat it or not. My parents explained to me it gave off a nice smell and was a sort of decoration to brighten up the place, and I couldn't get my head round that. These folk are shelling out cash for things to make their place smell nice?

Fuck me. Am I living in the botanical gardens? I was used to the aroma of stale cigarettes, alcohol and vomit as that had filled all my previous homes. It was a real mind bender but that was the area I was in.

The other kids around me were living in similar homes but they were getting into the more traditional sports like football, rugby and golf, whereas I was the outcast, always sprawled across my BMX. We might have lived in the same postcode but we weren't looking for the same things in life. The other youngsters hadn't seen what I had, nor had to crave freedom and security. That's what my Piranha represented.

Plus, it was the only piece of property that I could really say was mine. Well, that and my panda bear – which I had taken with me to my new home. But I had made my reputation by cracking people's noses apart with my skull so I wasn't advertising that I enjoyed cuddling this wee snuggly panda at night.

Even though I had my BMX I wasn't into tricks. I had seen a few but I had no idea how to do them. It was a commuter bike to me but I just felt so comfortable on it – the BMX thing suited me. I can't explain why, it's just something that appeals to every fibre of my being. It was flexible – you could bounce over mounds of dirt or slam down off the pavement, it was whatever you made it.

So while I was the black sheep of the locality, I did start to integrate even more as my school and parents made a big effort with my speech and because of my patchy education so far, I couldn't read or write properly. I was at least several years behind my age group and I'd struggle with words and stumble when speaking. I'd be cringing at trying to say 'lorry' as I knew how it should sound. But I could only get to 'lolly'. Some kids would look at me like I was daft as they didn't know why I had such poor speech.

My written sentences didn't make sense and I had made some complete howlers when it came to spelling. And of course, they laughed, but did it last? What do you think? My love of breaking bones would rise to the surface if I felt I was being isolated or made fun of as I still had that rogue element in me. It was mainly latent but it could appear if the correct conditions prevailed so me being laughed at didn't happen.

Reacting to any difficulty with anger and violence, or the threat of, was just my way of coping. In fact, I was really embarrassed inside. I had seen from my parents that there was a better way to live, the right way. I wanted that deep down but the thing was, I was struggling to get there – although that never put my parents off. They kept on helping and supporting me. No matter what it was, they were there to back me up and help me out and they would leave me alone outside of that, just to be free on my BMX.

This dynamic carried on for about 18 months and I gradually became more and more normal. The fights and anger issues kept subsiding and get this, I'd even mastered the art of chewing my food with my mouth shut – that was a bloody big achievement for me.

My sister Agnes was getting on well too but we were still Craigs – that was until my parents proposed to us. It was like a nervous teenager looking forward to prom night and then making a play for the girl of his dreams. They sat us down at home and told us very calmly that they'd like to make things official. So instead of being there as foster children, their idea was to formally adopt us. That was always their intention, but the rules stated you had to foster first, before making it permanent.

It's surreal when you think about it; these two kids who don't have a pot to piss in being asked by this amazingly kind and generous couple if they would do them the honour of becoming their kids. Logic dictates two things. It should have been the other way around – and it should have taken a nanosecond to say yes. But my fucking bad streak still hadn't been totally flushed out and it shot to the surface as the hairs on my neck stood up.

I kept my anger inside but my mind was racing, thinking there's no fucking way was I losing my name Craig. I hated my birth parents – my biological dad for being a waste of space and my biological mum for showing us the door and abandoning us. I had been gone from them for about five years by this point – three in Glenrosa and two in idyllic Kelvinside. But I didn't want this weird name, Buultjens. No way was I going to look like a dick by having to use that name – it sounded like something to clean an oven with.

It was all my own insecurity, again not feeling worthy or worrying about fitting in. I wouldn't have admitted it back then but that was what it was all about. My parents even told me a funny story later in life that when they asked me about the adoption I said to them, 'Does that mean I can live with you until I'm 40?' So I clearly knew where my bread was buttered!

And it's not like I had any reason to feel any loyalty to my biological family as even my brother used to let me down a lot. Eldridge and Marianna would drive me across to Drumchapel to see him as they were keen for us to keep in contact and not become strangers. And like most little brothers, I looked up to my older bro. He would get up to all sorts and I admired that for what I know now were the wrong reasons.

But we'd drive up and he wouldn't be there – quite simply, he didn't give a shit. He'd be out getting pissed with his pals and didn't want to be babysitting a wee guy. So my parents would pace back to the car and make up some excuse to cushion the blow. They would be trying to protect me, this wee boy, who they knew just wanted love. Instead of giving me the truth and strengthening their case for the adoption, they played it poker straight. They would pretend he had to go do something at the last minute.

My parents really did – and do – have the patience of saints. It was only later in life that Thomas confided in me that he purposely missed those meetings and deliberately tried to not be around me, so I didn't copy him. He'd realised that he was too far gone off the rails and saw no way back from the antisocial lifestyle of his, where things like stealing, getting into trouble and substance abuse had become the norm. So he was trying to do me a favour, but at that age I didn't see it like that.

Meanwhile, my parents let things lie by not trying to persuade us or talk about the adoption, and instead quietly carried on with the process in the background. After the paperwork had been completed and the information filed we all ended up in Glasgow's Sheriff Court in the city centre.

You hear people say it all the time, that they've come to a crossroads in their lives. It's a metaphor but I actually lived it as a reality. On the right we had Marianna and Eldridge Buultjens, all smart, prim and proper – sitting there full of dignity, class and respect. And on the left we had Thomas and Margaret Craig. They weren't as smart, they weren't turned out as well and looked like they were from a different world, which they were. My biological dad had become a shell of himself thanks to the stoke, but he was there.

After some legal proceedings and talking by lawyers and state workers, it came down to me. I was 12. The judge made it crystal clear that I had to make my choice and it wasn't to be made tucked away in some back room or some children's unit. He wanted it right there and then – in front of everyone.

I remember turning around and looking back at the court. On one side I'm looking at love, affection and care and on the other, I was staring at abuse, starvation and poverty.

Like I've explained, the old me had gradually been fizzling out and fading away. This was the exact point that he disappeared as I knew who I had to go with and even more importantly, who I wanted to be with – Marianna and Eldridge.

I became John Buultjens and John Craig died forever in that courtroom. He no longer existed, not on paper and not in flesh or blood. And you know what, thank fuck. I was glad to see the back of him.

It wasn't my fault but I didn't like what I was – that sort of self-hating and disgust had caused all my problems. Now I could drop all that baggage, breathe in some fresh air and fully engage in my new life. My biological mother erupted in floods of tears as my decision rang out across the silent room, her face crumpled up and she was clearly wounded – but I didn't feel bad. Most sons never wanted to hurt their mother, never mind see her cry. But I didn't have that connection to her in that way. I didn't enjoy her pain but at the same time, I felt no compulsion to run over and comfort her. I was no longer her son.

I felt a connection to my new parents that the couple I was born to never managed to create. They weren't able to be proper parents for whatever reasons – some innate and some of their own doing but my new parents could.

Agnes was only seven, so she never got to decide like me, but she was part of the deal too. I can recall vividly how I felt, and there was no pressure or beads of sweat trickling down my forehead. I was cool, calm and collected. It was the only choice to make.

Without my parents I'd have fuck all. Everything I've gone on to achieve is down to them – they are great, great people. And it was easily and remains still the best decision I've ever made. Not like that fuck-up with my first BMX and being blinded by those tacky mag wheels. At least I called the more important decision correctly.

RIDE

And now that I was a Buultjens I started to dig into my parents and find out about them, particularly my dad, as I'd always shied away from finding out too much due to my horrendous racism.

But now that shit had all gone he told me about how he'd been born in Colombo, the capital of Sri Lanka, and that his family had a good life there. They had a nanny for the kids, cash to spend, a nice house – it was a very comfortable lifestyle, but his father passed away when he was five. And his mother felt that dad and his brother Dev needed a strong education to set them up for their lives ahead.

So they left and moved to London in 1963. My dad took to the books and ended up as a research scientist after graduating from University of Manchester Institute of Science and Technology (UMIST). He'd then gone to Edinburgh University to do a post-grad in animal genetics and during that, met my mother. Dad then became part of the famous Beatson Institute at the University of Glasgow, which is still going strong as one of the world's leading centres in battling cancer and researching new treatments.

But in 1985 his time there was up and he was keen to move on and my mum was by this time working in Edinburgh at Holyrood College. She'd commute every day for about an hour and 15 minutes in the car down the M8, the motorway that connects Scotland's two biggest cities. So it's doable, but not ideal with two kids to get organised in the morning.

Anyway, my dad got two job offers that appealed to him. The first was in Sydney, the other side of the world with its all-year sunshine and beaches. And the second was in Dundee, which is a small city in eastern Scotland. It's on the Firth of Tay, which leads out to the North Sea, and it's a pretty rainy place, not known for being too adventurous. It's most famous son is probably Desperate Dan, the character from the iconic comic *The Dandy* – there's even a statue of Dan with his massive chin in the town centre. It seems like a no-brainer.

But my dad was not choosing based on the fun and frolics. He's a fucking scientist. He wanted the most interesting and challenging work. So yep, Dundee it was.

The now six-strong Buultjens clan began packing up – our newest member was our dog Bonnie, who Agnes and I had badgered my parents to get after a friend of my sister's had a dog that gave birth to a litter of pups – and we got to choose the one we liked. Both the pets were a smart move by my mum and dad, as it helped my sister and I integrate even more into the family unit.

By this time I had moved on from primary school to North Kelvinside Secondary but, as we were set to move, my spell there only last for two academic years.

What stuck with me was the words of my maths teacher ringing in my ears. I can't recall his name but he was a hairy bastard and looked like a bear. He told me, 'John, you'll amount to nothing.' It was when I was sitting down to choose my subjects for the following years and what path I'd be following. Christ knows why he thought it was a good idea to tell a teenager that. I'll never forget it though.

While I was no straight-A student, I had been doing my BMX homework diligently and I'd managed to nail my first trick. Most people never forget their first kiss but for a BMXer it's the first move they manage to nail to the extent that they can do it whenever the mood takes them.

I popped my cherry with the endo, which in the grand scheme of things is pretty simple really, but it was pioneered by my main man at the time, Bob Haro, so it was a cataclysmic event for me. It's basically a nose wheelie, so you hammer away at speed, slam on the front brake and let the back wheel go right up in the air. Tom Cruise did it in one of the *Mission Impossible* movies so I'm in good company there.

Just as the summer holidays were coming up, I made the announcement to my class that I wouldn't be back next year. They all erupted with laughter and were telling me, 'You're off to choochter land.' A choochter is a Scottish term for someone who doesn't come from the central belt – and is intended to demean them, kind of paint them as backward and not too sophisticated. A bit like calling someone trailer trash.

The other thing was my mates reckoned I'd be shagging sheep, even though Dundee is a fully built-up place and not close to The Highlands at all. But that's another Scottish obsession. Anyone from north of the central belt is automatically assumed to be obsessed with sheep – and with so little to do, they must end up having sex with them to spice up their dull, rural lives.

I'll just get in early with this one – in all my time in Dundee, I never shagged a sheep.

# 5

# Dundee

IT'S only 65 miles away, but Dundee is a completely different kettle of fish from Glasgow. Scotland is a small country but each part of it has its own ideas about the others. Our family settled into our new home at 10 Roxburgh Terrace in 1986, and I rocked up at Harris Academy – which was to be my final school. They expected me to be a hard case because Glasgow has the reputation of producing people who take no shit, like to fight and drink a lot.

The irony was that it was exactly what I used to be but I was trying my damnedest to not be that. In fact, I wasn't having to try as since the adoption, John Buultjens was a persona I was enjoying and revelling in. But as I turned up at Harris, some of the lads wanted to take me on – sort out the cheeky, cocky Glasgow wide boy, as they saw me. So I thought, 'Fuck it, I can go through my days having wee fights or scraps, or I can nip it in the bud.'

And as at most schools there was a hierarchical ranking of who was the best fighter. In my year group there was this guy called Graham Bell, known in the halls as 'Bagsy'. So I marched right up to him one day and said, 'Fucking right now, square go.' Again for any non-Glaswegians, a square go is a challenge to fight. He was a big bastard, a good foot taller than me, but I was fucking up for it.

I just wanted to do him and then put all this crap to bed. Bagsy looked a bit puzzled and then his face cracked into a wide smile, he went, 'You're a crazy wee fucker,' and put his arm around me.

So that was it. He'd accepted me and I'd showed everyone I had the balls to take him on. So no one stepped to me again at Harris.

But my academic performance wasn't quite as simple. I was shite. Part of it was that I'd had such an awful schooling in my early days, that I was always playing catch-up. Another reason was I wasn't interested. Pythagoras's theorem; the periodic table; Shakespeare and Chekhov, more like fuck off.

I even failed biology and that really devastated my dad. The biology teacher knew of my dad being at the university as he was a respected academic and a PhD. So he was giving me the big build-up at the start of the year, announcing to the class who I was and how lucky we were to have someone from such an esteemed family. And then it was a big fucking embarrassment as I crashed and burned.

My mother didn't take it as hard but for my dad, being raised to regard education as important, he couldn't help but be frustrated at my performance. We'd sit at home and he'd be making things simple, doing equations like $X + Y = Z$ over and over. But simply the only X I gave a hoot about was BMX. The thing is I'm not daft. I've got a brain, but it doesn't work if I'm not interested. Weirdly, if I like something I'll soak it up like a sponge.

I can name you angles, dimensions, colour schemes of bikes going back decades. No problem. I can churn out spiels from movies that I liked, I remember the quotes exactly and how they were delivered.

In my current role now running Haro BMX I have to make decisions involving millions of dollars. It's impacting things across 80 countries but I do it all in my head. My accountant looks at me like I've landed from Mars but I tell him that it's all in my mind. I know what we have to spend and how to allocate it. I do it all mentally so I'm no dumb-ass. I've actually been called an intellectual by some people, and that's not something I ever heard at school.

In fact, after two years at Harris, I was shown the door. Actually, I was politely asked to leave. It's the old one when a sports team manager is sacked by the owner but the official line is that they offered their resignation.

The end came for me after a session with the guidance counsellor. I was coming to the end of the fourth year and in Scotland, you pick your subjects for the next two years, to go for a place in university. So the counsellor asked me what I was into. I wanted to say girls but I kept it proper and said, 'I like to ride my bike.' And no, they didn't suggest me becoming a BMX pro.

I also had flashbacks to my old teacher in Glasgow saying, 'John, you'll amount to nothing.' It was all a bit awkward as they were sitting there trying to analyse what direction to send me in, going on that all I'd said was that I was into BMX and not much else. But then through the silence and awkwardness, I offered that I actually didn't mind baking.

You see, during my time in Dundee I'd kept on going with the riding. A lot of people would see me and shout things like, 'When are you going to stop riding that kids' bike?' It was never too bad and not to my face after I proved my mettle with Bagsy. But they did think I was a bit of a weirdo; they were going to discos and the more typical older teenage things, and I was flying about on a BMX.

I also went through a good few bikes by this time as I was constantly buying and trading either at bike shops or through catalogues. I had myself a classy Mongoose and then I even got a DP Freestyler – the difference was that I no longer expected my parents to fund it. I wanted to do right by them and with my shocking school record, I was hardly in a position to be asking for large sums of cash to update my bike.

I initially had a paper round but that wasn't the most stimulating. Then I spotted that a bakery called The Gateau Parlour was looking for someone to help out on the weekends. It was an early start, about 4am, and I just had to go in and get things ready as all of the baking had been done. I was doing things like scooping the mince into the pies and putting the tops on. The guy running it had a good heart and even started to teach me how to do stuff like making choux pastry. And the best thing about the whole gig was that I was done by lunchtime, so I could grab my bike and get riding.

By this time I'd nailed the rock walk which is the same as an Endo but when your wheel is up, you spin around 180 degrees and slam it down, then bring it up again and spin back around 180. I began taking on other jumps and tricks now too. Okay, we're not talking anything big-time, but I was having a go.

It was mainly because BMX was really growing around the world, so I was going into the newsagents and seeing magazines. I was eating these things up and devouring every word; they were like propaganda to me. They were commandments on how to live life.

Videos were also starting to appear and things were shown on TV. So while it was not a big thing in Dundee I could sense it was going on across the planet – and I was part of it, in my own small way.

I didn't really have any skills though. I hadn't had a chance to develop them as I'd not even been on a ramp. But then my dad sorted that out. He had a colleague at the university who was from Hawaii. Again, what the fuck is it with these academics, who leaves Hawaii for Dundee? What the fuck, God give me strength!

Anyway I'm grateful he did, as his son Darryl Smith was into skateboarding. The dads must have got talking and reckoned we'd be a good fit – and we were. We got on like a house on fire as we were both sort-of outcasts due to our passions being different from most boys at our age. One Saturday Darryl brought me down to Broughty Ferry, a suburb to the east of Dundee, and they had a proper ten-foot ramp there. I looked at this thing, which I'd only ever seen in magazines, and thought 'fucking yes'.

I guess it's the equivalent of some teenage boys meeting Jenna Jameson but I couldn't go on it. Not for a lack of guts, but I didn't know what the fuck I was doing. They had, however, started to build a smaller, four-foot ramp, so that became my routine every Saturday. Bed. Bakery. BMX. Broughty Ferry.

It was a fair trek on a BMX with no gears. It's about an hour and 20 minutes each way and often I did it in the pissing rain but all the effort was well worth it when one day I spotted Scott Carroll there. He was Scottish and had just won the BMX World Championship for his age group. I didn't know he hung out there and lived locally – and I was in awe as I saw him firing up and down the big ramp. Here was the best rider in the world, in front of my very own eyes.

Quite simply, I wanted to be Scott. The way he carried himself, the way he dressed, the way he looked; it was as cool as fuck. He wore a few Swatch watches on each wrist and I swore to myself I was going to jump on that bandwagon too. So yep, you guessed it. A portion of my Gateau Parlour green was going on watches while the rest was being pumped into my bike. As soon as I had nine, I wore them like he did – if you look closely on the cover of this book you'll see some of them.

I even contemplated getting blond tints in my hair, like Scott, but I am a ginger bastard and it wasn't going to look good – I wasn't that daft. For ages though I watched from afar. He'd be doing all sorts of complicated manoeuvres and flying through the air whereas I was struggling to master simpler things. But I kept going back and back and back and back – I was determined to do it like him. I know it sounds weird but it was all I wanted to do, even at 16. It was that much fun for me.

And I kept practising even more until the point I mastered my first real tricky stunt – the abubaca. It involves firing up the ramp at full pelt, jumping up into the air and landing your back tyre on the metal coping, which is the edge between the wooden sections. I had such a rush when I finally nailed it.

The skill came in as it was an all-or-nothing manoeuvre. Half an inch too far forward and you're on your arse; half an inch short and your face is smashing into that steel edge. Once you're on the coping, you hold it for just a split second – and then fly backwards, totally blind and drop back into the ramp.

Just thinking about it gives me a boner. The feeling of pulling it off never got old – and still doesn't today.

What a rush. Better than sex? I'd have to say it depends who it was with.

And while going to Broughty Ferry to do all this was a thrill, it wasn't possible during the week so me and another budding rider I'd met, Iain Carnegie, decided to get serious and build our own ramp. It was a piece of utter shit as we'd put it together using old wooden pallets.

It was unstable and would fall apart all the time as we didn't have a clue what we were doing, so we started having a real good look at how Scott's was constructed. It was all cut to fit with pieces known as transitions. We realised we needed better materials but they were out of our reach so we soldiered on with our sub-standard construction for weekdays only.

And my money from the bakery meant I could keep adding to my bike or upgrading, even if it was just a new brake cable or a better set of pegs – and I could also splash out for any critical repairs to our ramp. No stealing, no guilt and all under my own steam, so it was a win-win situation.

Anyway, when I mentioned all this to the counsellor, they awoke from their slumber and suggested I get myself over to local Kingsway Technical College as they were running a four-week introductory course on cooking.

I don't think they gave a shit if it was going to work out for me but at least I'd be out of their hair and out of the school.

So I left and embarked on a career in the kitchen – with my mind still consumed by everything and anything that involved BMX.

* * * * *

I loved BMX and I wasn't giving up, even though I had done a month trying to be the next Gordon Ramsay – which then led to another year of basic cooking courses. And eventually Scott must have taken pity on me as he'd come over to the four-foot ramp. He could see how much the sport meant to me and the commitment I was putting in, spending hours trying to do simple tricks and not getting them.

So he'd start giving me little tips, telling me do it this way or try it that way. Meanwhile I was still getting help from other top riders like Mat Hoffman and Dennis McCoy over in America – through the magazines I kept buying religiously. The irony is, I used to idolise them. Now Dennis rides for me at Haro and we're close pals. Fucking hell, what a trip.

But back then it was another universe and while serving my apprenticeship, I needed more money to get a better bike. I needed to either get myself a Haro or a GT. They were the McCartney and Lennon of the BMX world – both were top-class and I finally had enough in the piggy bank to afford a serious top-of-the range bike so I got my Haro Sport in 1988.

Scott looked at me differently the first day I showed up on it – and so did the rest of the boys. I was part of the gang now, no longer just wee wannabe John. It was time to hit the big ramp and I was up for the challenge, and then some. I had begun dabbling with Scott's signature move, the rock walk drop-in, which is the same as doing it on the ground but you do it on the top of the ramp and then fall in blind. It looks fucking easy but it's not and if you mess it up, you're flat on your face – even more embarrassing if you're riding a Haro and do that. It's a bit like driving a red convertible Ferrari, blasting out dance music on the stereo and then stalling at the traffic lights in front of a load of pedestrians.

That bike also fostered a lifelong friendship with an Italian lad called Andrea Piana. I'd spied these exotic-looking Italian girls in Dundee one day and being a gentleman I rode over at speed to see if I could perhaps be their personal tour guide.

But then this wee mouthy lad piped up and pointed at my Haro Sport, chuntering on about how he had a Haro GT back home. I think talking about Haro bikes was the only thing that could have taken my attention off those tanned goddesses – as you have to remember, I'd not seen much else at that point in my life apart from pasty Scottish folk, like myself. In the end we became pen pals and I actually took my first trip outside the UK to see him in Italy during the following New Year holidays.

I'd also begun to build up more pals from across the Dundee area, all of us connected by being unadulterated BMX nuts, so the likes of me, Iain, Alan Smith and

David Macdonald all hung around together. We'd all be at Scott's ramp and I had even started to get called 'John Carroll' by some wisecrackers – as they had spotted my obsession with Scott. I denied it but they were spot-on. I was even able to fire on Scott's big ramp too, so to any onlookers the only discernible difference between us was purely genetic at this point.

But I still hankered after my own big ramp so I wasn't always on Scott's turf – and luckily, the developer Barratt's had begun building houses in Dundee. Iain was on board with my construction project but we had to walk two miles to their development as we couldn't use the bikes – because we weren't coming back empty-handed!

We'd cut through the graveyard and the park because you couldn't be seen by a soul as it was pitch black, and then skip on to the site. This was before the days of security fences and CCTV. We'd grab ourselves 8x4 sheets of plywood and crossbeams, as much as we could carry – then retrace our steps.

Iain's dad took pity on us one day as he didn't know where the wood was coming from but he offered to drive me and Iain to B&Q – who sell every sort of tool and building material under the sun. We were a pair of crafty buggers and we only picked one sheet of wood. Iain's dad was like, 'Are you sure that's all you want, boys?'

'Oh yes, that's it,' we both chimed back. He didn't know we weren't wanting to pay and were actually stealing our supplies. So we loaded the van and he drove us back to our ramp. Call it divine intervention or plain luck, but Iain's old man was a smoker and he happened to be out of fags. And as you do, he stopped at a Spar to get some. Didn't it just happen to be right opposite the building site that we'd been pilfering. I glanced at Iain. He looked at me – and it was on.

We shot out of that fucking van like a pair of Exocet missiles, both of us grabbing as much as we could carry. I'm convinced the adrenaline pumping through my veins turned me into the Incredible Hulk. Iain and I had the van full in a matter of minutes. We jumped back in and as his dad came back, we were casually chilling – desperately trying to mask the heavy breathing and beads of sweat smeared across our faces. I've always wondered if Iain's dad noticed and I feel he must have as surely he could feel the weight driving a van full of wood, compared to one with a single sheet. He never mentioned it. So if you're reading this, sorry Mr Carnegie, you were an accessory to robbery without knowing it.

The operation allowed us to finally have that decent ramp of our own and with my skills rapidly improving I was at a proper level with my Haro bike as the foundation, so I began entering contests. I'd sometimes travel with Scott and the other guys all over the UK to compete.

But that wasn't ever my attitude really. I didn't care if I won or not – not because I didn't want to nail my routine, I did and I took it very seriously, but I just loved doing it for the sheer thrill. Being a pro rider and doing it for money wasn't on my radar. I think then that me being paid for it would have been sacrilege, a bit like getting paid to help your frail old grandparents cut their grass – something about it didn't quite sit right with me. I was just there to have a blast and ride my heart out.

All of the BMX crews liked me. I was welcomed in and again it wasn't because of my skills. Plenty of them at this point could do way more than me but I had guts, I was a maverick. They'd see this ginger blur careering up the ramp into some move that I had at best a 60-40 chance of pulling off. But I didn't give a fuck. I'd lived a nightmare and now I had the dream scenario and I was going to rip it up. I went from being a mainstream outcast to getting some serious street BMX cred.

Protection was uncool so none of us bothered with that. My only concession was that eventually I got a pair of shin pads as the pedals were really chewing up my shins but spilling blood wasn't going to get close to coming in the way of me living out my BMX dreams.

# 6

# Angus Thistle

AFTER Kingsway Tech had spat me out I knew what my next move was. Australia had caught my eye. My mum's family had moved out there and kept sending us postcards and pictures of exotic scenes that I'd only seen in movies. My dad's brother, uncle Dev, had also made the move there many years ago, so I had plenty of connections.

It looked superb. Sunshine, beaches, barbecues, it was paradise to me. But that was mainly because I figured in that climate I could do even more riding. I wouldn't have to sit out days when we had snow and ice, an all-too-common occurrence in Scotland. I could be out there giving it plenty morning to night.

Eventually the Aussie correspondence tipped the balance and I decided that I was going there. I did a little bit of research and my family were able to sponsor me. But I had to have more qualifications to my name than my one-year college course so I kept my ear to the ground around Dundee for a way out of the cul-de-sac I was in, and I managed to start working as a functions waiter at The Angus Thistle Hotel. They'd come up to the college and let us all know they were looking for part-time workers.

Once my course was over, though, I needed to get more cash coming in so I made the jump to working as a breakfast waiter where I'd be carrying out the porridge, toast, and whatever else people ordered. To be honest it kept my mum and dad sweet as I was no layabout – and the cherry on the cake was it allowed me to keep riding on the ramps whenever I had spare time. But I didn't last long before I was fired. The reason? BMX, ironically.

I was up until all hours riding as much as I could so I was in no fit state to be bright-eyed and bushy tailed to start a shift at 5am – or quite often I was nursing a broken bone and couldn't get to work. One time I hobbled in after appearing at the King Of Concrete, which takes place in the English seaside resort of Southsea. I gave it some serious oomph and went for a 720-degree jump. But as I spun around I under-rotated and came down at an angle, losing my balance and crashing to the ground.

I'd begun wearing knee pads now and then – trying to be all sensible. This day I had them on, so as I went down hard I felt glad that at least my knees wouldn't be ripped up and a bloody mess. Well, thankfully they weren't. But as my knees hit the concrete the rivets that fixed the cushioning to the plastic drove right through it and into my bones. The three rivets caused my patella to snap on my right knee and left me with a hairline fracture in my left.

Instantly both of them swelled up like balloons but I kept riding and did a few more jumps as I was there to compete – not to give up after a fall.

Me and the boys at this time also began filming ourselves doing jumps and tricks. It was the era of when the camcorder and home movies were all the rage, VHS of course, but everyone seemed to be fascinated by it. As a big gang of riders we started calling ourselves Pilgrim, a name actually thought up after I was arrested by the police.

I was mortified as it was the first time since cleaning up my act that I'd had any trouble with the boys in blue. They collared me after they stormed the square outside the city's Caird Hall. That's where we used to congregate; the BMXers, skateboarders, and all of us who were into that type of stuff.

At the time I was riding my new Dyno Slammer that I'd imported from the States. I'd be coming off the concrete ledges, jumping the plant pots and grinding on the stairs – like all the other guys and girls were. But when the police rushed into the square, they only managed to nab me and my mate John-Paul Mathews, who was skating. The rest of them fled like thieves in the night.

So I ended up back at Dundee's Bell Street police station and my parents were called down. It was all pretty serious. They even impounded my bike, which really pissed me off, as I'd had it delivered from Trend Bike Source in Texas – and it was my pride and joy.

I was charged with three offences; Breach of the Peace, Damaging Public Property and Endangering Pedestrians. It was a lot of crap but they let me go and informed me I'd be notified of my court date. What really had me worried was the lack of a bike as I'd been due to go to Barrow-in-Furness down in England that weekend to see my mate Craig Rawlings.

I managed to borrow a bike from a pal though, so I made the trip. I did OK in the contest but it wasn't my BMX, so I didn't perform as well as I could have. But I did catch the eye of a girl from Stoke on Trent, ironically called Celina Stokes. We met at the cinema and she liked my dress style – and we hit it off.

The next day we were riding the ramp and Celina came to see us strut our stuff, but her ex-boyfriend turned up and didn't like that Celina was keen on me. He waded over and smacked me across the face with a cricket bat. I was ready to leather him but then I realised he had a whole team of guys with him, so even with a few local pals with me we were seriously outnumbered 10-1. We had to leg it as they were baying for blood and seemed to want to embarrass us for coming down to their skatepark and impressing with our skills.

Somehow the four of us, including Celina, squashed into a Mini Cooper. I don't know how we did, and how we got our bikes in too. I vaguely recall Craig's friend took them in his car but it was all so much of a blur as we scattered. We screeched off like we were in a movie and ended up in some open field, but my face was bloody pounding as he'd really cracked me good.

Celina was comforting me and we ended up shagging in the back of Craig's Mini later that night, so she certainly soothed my pain. It seemed to be a common end to sticky situations for me.

I did end up back at that same skatepark for another visit as I'd been going up and down to see Celina. Again, I was not on my bike as the cops still had it, and the one I was using wasn't configured for me. My first run went badly as I ended up falling during a 360 over the spine and snapped my fibula.

I had to go to hospital so Craig drove me and my foot was shaking everywhere – the pain was unbearable. I needed surgery and the doctor explained I could have it done in Stoke-on-Trent or back in Dundee. I thought being closer to home was a better plan so they sent me on my way on the train with a temporary cast and a heap of morphine to dull the agony. The train pulled in to Dundee later that night where my folks were waiting for me and it was straight to Dundee Royal Infirmary.

The next day I had a metal plate and 14 screws inserted into my fibula, all of which are still there 25 years later. Weirdly I also still have my plaster cast with all my boys' signatures on it – so that's one happy souvenir at least! Don't ask me why but I kept it, and my parents later shipped it out with a bunch of my things to my new home in Australia.

Anyway, time rumbled on and I was summoned to court in Dundee. I think my parents almost keeled over when it was read out that the cops calculated I'd done damage to the sum of £500,000. The police brought up forensic evidence of concrete on my bike, being the same as the concrete in the square. For fuck's sake. It was like they were trying Al Capone. I was a BMX kid having some fun with his pals.

Thankfully the Procurator Fiscal – Scotland's prosecution service – saw that and told them to get lost. All the charges were dismissed and I was a free man and even sweeter, my bike had to be released. So I went down to collect it but I was still injured and I limped into the reception and signed all the paperwork – they released it, and thankfully it was still in mint condition.

But the officers were laughing their heads off as they saw me pedalling away. I could barely move my bone so it was a one-legged job as I swooped all over the place, left then right. But I got home and the Slammer was back where it belonged.

All of that is why our crew took the name Pilgrim. It was a reaction to feeling downtrodden and being judged. So we began using the name and using it in the videos we filmed. One of the clips even saw me appear on *You've Been Framed* and interviewed by its host Jeremy Beadle.

I'd been on a ramp at my old pal Alan Smith's house and wanted to show him a new trick, which went horribly wrong as I lost control of my bike and went crashing through his garden fence. It collapsed like a pack of cards and I was left on my backside. It was your classic home video gaffe and I got my first bit of national TV exposure, and was even invited into the studio.

If you get online, there's still a clip of me sitting there with Beadle – in a rather fetching Anarchic Adjustment baseball cap turned backwards. Come on, it was the early 90s after all!

Although The Angus had fired me, once I'd healed up I wasn't out of the place for long as the functions manager rang me and brought me back in to rejoin their team. So at least I had an income as I devised a way to get myself – and my bike – 9,500 miles across the globe.

The major sticking point was that in order to obtain the visa, I needed a proper qualification behind me. I didn't have that because I'd left school early and my cooking course at the Kingsway wasn't going to cut the mustard with the Australian immigration department. But the functions manager had taken a liking to me and told me about the assistant trainee management programme the hotel was running. It was a four-year course with a guaranteed degree at its conclusion. But at the end I could go to Australia and be welcomed in with open arms. I was never in a million years going to get into any university, never mind leave with a degree, so it was my only shot and I went for it. In for a penny, in for a pound and all that.

It involved becoming acquainted with all parts of the hotel. Every six months I was put into different departments and then rotated around. It was so the management team understood what each part of the hotel was doing, not just by watching but by actually getting their hands dirty. I really liked it and I was on reception checking guests in, manning the bar, in the laundry washing bed linen and all sorts, and then in the kitchen too. I didn't mind the kitchen but as luck would have it, I was back doing the early shift. Fucking breakfasts again. Manning the frying pan at 4.30 every morning during that stint was hell on earth, not the work but the early rises.

Jesus Christ, I did feel a bit daft having done all that graft to end up back where I had started, but instead of carrying the plates, I was filling them up. Scrambled eggs, bacon, sausages, black pudding, haggis, it was all that stuff. Nothing to have Gordon Ramsay shaking in his boots, but it was solid grub.

The thing was that the early mornings were progressively a killer and with our own big ramp, I was spending as much time down there as possible, so I'd be getting home late – often close to midnight – and then having to be up again in four hours. Maybe the lack of sleep contributed to turning up in a real state a few times.

The worst was as I flew down Blackness Road like a bat out of hell, trying to get there before my boss noticed, and I took on a green pyramid which sticks out of the ground. It's actually the roof covering the public toilets underneath. Now it has a small fence around it but back in those days that wasn't there.

I would deliberately seek out obstacles to make the ride more fun and challenging and this morning I launched off it but I was going too fast, overshot it and smashed straight into a brick wall. I was banged up pretty bad but managed to struggle on to work. The head chef breezed in to check on how the breakfasts were coming along, and looked in disgust as he saw me standing there covered in blood. He didn't say anything but his disapproving look was enough.

Another time I was riding across a roundabout, granted not the best thing to be doing on a cold, dark morning – especially with no lights on my bike. I messed up my jump and ended up landing in front of the oncoming traffic. I slammed into the side of a very smart-looking Mercedes and the pegs on my bike scrapped right down its sleek body. I had dinged it up and made a hell of a mess.

The driver sprang out and I braced myself for a demand for financial reparation, which I didn't have. But he was more worried about me and I just palmed him off as all I could see was the damage to his big fancy motor. I rode off into the darkness and never heard another word about it. The guy really was a gentleman as he'd have been well within his rights to demand that I paid up.

Getting to work was always an adventure and even if it wasn't, I turned it into one. Thankfully the breakfast rotation ended and I was finally away from the fucking bacon and eggs. The worst thing was that hotels are open 24 hours a day and as an assistant manager, overtime was not an option.

So I'd be putting in 100-hour weeks and my pay packet every Friday was only £100 – and this was up until 1994. I was basically getting less than the minimum wage but it's what the programme demanded. Beggars on the street were making more than me. And that's not just hyperbole, I saw it first-hand – so I certainly wasn't doing any of it for the money.

But all the time I kept thinking, 'Hold it together and you'll be riding your BMX in the glorious sunshine soon.' I actually quite enjoyed the toughness. I've always like things hard, which I think is to do with my early years in Whiteinch, Drumchapel and Glenrosa. If things are too easy, I don't feel I've earned them as I never wanted things handed to me on a plate.

Plus I wanted to prove to my mum and dad that I could do something with my life. And without blowing my own trumpet, I excelled as the hotel game fits with how I take things in. Like I've said, I was shit academically and wasn't one to tackle the textbooks but the hotel was all about doing it. So when it came to my assessments or exams, I sailed through as I'd done it and that was enough. If I do something and commit to it, then I grasp it no problem.

I'm working on this part of the book while I'm in Fargo in North Dakota. It was made famous by the movies and the big TV show. But a few hours ago, I did a talk in front of 49 store managers who sell about $2.5m of Haro bikes. And I didn't bring any notes or do any preparation. I don't have to. I lived BMX, I've lived the bikes, I've been on them, I've taken them apart – the only thing I haven't done is sleep with them and you never know, I might start that one day!

It was the same at the hotel. I had lived the roles so being tested on them was a walk in the park. I also had plenty of fun at The Angus including one great time when we met the famous Alessi twins from the soap *Neighbours* – which at this point was at fever-pitch levels of popularity.

They were doing a promotional tour and were booked in overnight. I had fantasised over one of the twins, Caroline – her real name is Gillian Blakeney. I don't know why it was about her so much as Gayle was clearly no different – but hey-ho.

I was standing there trying to play it cool while looking at them in the lobby but my old heart was going like the clappers. I finally plucked up the courage to ask them if they fancied coming across to the local boozer for a drink. But they were heading out, or that's what they told me anyway, so I asked for a photo with them outside the hotel – and they also gave me one of their signed promotional cards, which I showed off to my friends for weeks.

I also especially recall the night when The Prodigy were staying. They were out promoting their debut album and were doing a gig at Fat Sam's in Dundee. I knew their music and checked them in at reception, and somehow I mentioned I was hoping to go to the show, but it was sold out. Taking pity on me, they stuck me on the guest list and said to come backstage.

I didn't need to be asked twice and showed up, really enjoyed the gig and I went back to the hotel with them. We used to have an old guy, Tom Donaldson, who did the night shift. He let us all in and the drinks were flowing in the bar, and then the guys in the band rolled a joint.

Soon it was being passed around and this was the first time I ever got stoned. I was out of my tree but I'll always remember Tom passing by, picking up some empty glasses and mentioning something about the strange cigarette we were smoking – he didn't have a clue it was marijuana.

Eventually the party came to an end and I was on my bike as usual, cycling home around 2am. But because I was completely wasted I bounced off a smallish kerb, lost my balance and ended up flat on my back in the middle of the road, looking up at the stars. That's all I can recall and I've no idea how I finally made it home.

So even though I had gone corporate – well, sort of – I was still riding any time I could and using every minute of my days off to hone my skills and the tricks were now starting to come to me.

And I kept hammering away at the coal face in The Angus Thistle as I was going to Australia by one way or another.

One perk my employment did allow me to call in, was the hotel let me have the ballroom for my 21st-birthday bash. It was an epic affair with 540 people packed in and was organised by one of the most enchanting females I've ever encountered, Morven Sinclair.

I'd met her the previous year at this big student end-of-term house party. I turned up as ever on my bike, I flew in like a madman and started riding up the walls of someone's house. The music was banging as my good pal Tom Simpson was manning the wheels of steel. Tom would go on to become a big-time musician and was part of Snow Patrol for their massive albums, when they became one of the world's biggest pop groups and released songs like 'Chasing Cars'. But that night, I suspected he had his eye on Morven too. And I can't blame him, she was like Bjork – really arty and different.

As soon as I caught sight of her, I thought, 'Who the fuck is that girl?' We hit it off but I didn't see her again for months as she'd gone back home to Elgin for the summer.

But I randomly came across her at our local, The Parliamentary Bar in Dundee, which led to us dating, and, being a great girlfriend during the course of our time together, she threw my 21st. Tom was part of a DJ crew called The Spaceship so he sorted out the music. He actually hand-drew the invitations and really put some thought into it. I still have one – it's a class piece of work. Another friend of mine, Nick DeCosemo, also played that night and he went on to become a big-name

DJ in his own right before moving into music magazines and publishing. So the guests got value for money I must say, two class acts for the price of a birthday present.

I've never actually seen Tom play with Snow Patrol although wherever I've been in the world, I've bought their albums to support them and as a wee thank you for making my birthday so special. It was a really great night although I lost touch with Morven, but I know that before me she had dated Stephen Hendry, who went on to become the seven-time world snooker champion. Maybe going out with a mad BMXer like me was her natural reaction to being with more of a laid-back sportsman. He did his thing in a dapper bow tie and waistcoat, I did mine in a pair of a shorts and a baseball cap.

Along with my 21st, that ballroom was also the scene where I was sexually assaulted by a member of the royal family. Well, maybe it wasn't a full-on assault. I was working at a function one night for a charity ball and my role was to serve the potatoes and green beans, so I had a huge silver dish on one arm with a napkin so I didn't get burnt, and in the other was the large serving spoon and fork.

Princess Margaret – who passed away in 2002 – was the guest of honour, which was a big deal as she was the Queen's only sibling. Plus she had a reputation of liking a good drink and smoked like a chimney, so was portrayed as being a bit of a rebel in royal circles. And just as I had put the portions on her plate, I turned to the right to do the next person at the table and I felt this short but firm pinch of my backside.

We made eye contact for an awkward few seconds – and then I carried on dishing out the veg. Making a move on royalty was a step too far, even for me.

* * * * *

Finally my time at The Angus was up and I had some real paperwork to my name – I was a graduate. Not in the PhD league of my dad, but at least I had something behind me and a proper career to fall back on.

As soon as it came through, I furiously scribbled out my Australian immigration forms. Everything was submitted and my relatives out there – my aunt Norah, who is my mum's sister, and her husband Roger – agreed to formally sponsor me. Basically that meant that if I ended up not finding work and making an arse of it, they'd look after me. A condition of the visa was that I couldn't claim social security but I was planning never to let it come to that, and vowed to make sure I provided for myself.

The only snag was that the Australian embassy told me it would be 12 months before my visa was ready. It was a bit of a kick in the teeth as I'd busted my balls in The Angus and I was all set to get the shorts on, jump on my bike and spend hours working on tricks and stunts in the sunshine. Now I had to find some way of filling the time. I didn't want to let my parents down either, as

I was conscious of how much they have done for me and also how hard it was for them to see their son make an arse of his education.

So I'd heard about a position at another hotel in the chain up in Aberdeen looking for an assistant manager. Since I had just rolled off the company's production line, I reckoned I had a good shot at getting it – and I did. I was off again but this time alone, to The Thistle in the part of the city known as Dyce, where the airport is situated. My plan was just to get my head down, save some money and get set for Oz.

But after my four-year intensive training course across every part of a bustling hotel, I only lasted two weeks in the Aberdeen role. It still makes my blood boil as it was a lot of effort for little in return. The reason was that the manager in Dyce was a complete arsehole. She seemed to have this chip on her shoulder and wanted to take it out on me every chance she could. She would demean me in front of the rest of the staff. It started the minute I walked in the main doors and into the lobby.

The straw that broke the camel's back was one evening when the beer kegs had leaked down in the cellar, so the floor was flooded and she called me to go down there and mop it all up. I'm no prima donna but stop the bus, I'd paid my dues, I had done all the shit jobs – I'd earned my stripes. I was supposed to be part of management so I called my good mate Grant Smith to come and get me and I never went back.

That weekend there was a BMX contest called Backyard Jam down in Hastings, on the south coast of England.

I knew I had to tell my parents and that they'd be gutted that I'd chucked away the only professional career option open to me. But I had to do what I thought was right and I put calling them off, joining the boys on the road trip south.

The contest was great. I enjoyed it and used it to let out some of the stress that was rattling about in my brain but on the way back, I nearly killed us all. We'd been splitting the driving as it takes about ten hours and on my turn behind the wheel, after the exertions on the ramps, my knee locked and pressed the pedal flat to the floor. The other guys, Grant, Peter Lindsay and Paul Robertson, were freaking out as the engine revved up and we kept getting faster and faster. 'Fuck, my bloody knee is frozen, I can't get my foot off the pedal,' I yelled.

Peter, without telling me, leaned over and yanked up the lever to unlock my seat and fired me backwards. As that happened of course, my arms couldn't reach the steering wheel, so we began veering off towards the motorway barrier but thankfully Paul in the passenger seat spotted the danger and straightened us up in the nick of time.

As we came to a spluttering halt, Grant took over and I was relived of all driving duties. I went for a sleep in the back of the van as I'd been on the go all weekend

– and I awoke to be parked outside my parents' house in Dundee.

My mates thought it would be hilarious for me to accost my mum and dad at 6am on Monday as they got ready for work and let them know my career in hospitality had been flushed down the toilet, like a giant turd. 'Fucking hell boys, get me out of here,' I said.

Peter finally drove off and I also made a mental note, 'Don't confide in your pals without caution as they sometimes like to see you suffer.'

While leaving the hotel group felt like the right thing to do as I wasn't going to be demeaned, it did give me a bit of a dilemma of how to spend the time until my visa arrived. Bikes seemed to be the way to go as it was the only thing – outside of my family – that I loved.

I heard through another friend, Paul Morrison, who worked at Alpine Bikes in Aberdeen, that they had a job going. They took me on as the owner could see how passionate I was about bikes. I didn't have to fake it, my life was BMX. The time flew by as I was having a ball. I was actually on a better wage than I was at the hotel – plus I didn't have to deal with the nightmare erratic shift pattern. In the shop, it was nine to five and a cheeky lunchtime finish on a Saturday.

I finally plucked up the courage to let my parents know on the phone and I could feel my dad's deep disappointment transmitting down the line. But once again both of them came up trumps for me. They didn't berate me or give me a rollocking.

I felt a bit like a 22-year-old acting like a 12-year-old, and wouldn't have felt aggrieved if they'd given me the hairdryer treatment. Instead they accepted it and told me that as long as I was happy, then that was enough for them. My parents were consistently keen for me to do what made me happy and that support always humbled me.

From then on in, life was sweet. I'd be selling all kinds of bikes in the shop and saving the money I could, spending the rest on getting a better BMX to ride – or buying upgraded parts to make my pride and joy better. And I'd plugged into a good social scene, so if we weren't all going to contests around the UK, we'd be partying and working on tricks together.

Then just as my year was coming to an end, the Australian embassy came good on their promise. My visa had been granted and I had three months to get my arse to the other side the world. What had only been a dream was now set to become a reality.

# 7

# Ramsay Street

S UNDAY, 11 JUNE 1995 was the date I left
Scotland. I was booked to fly in to Melbourne
and the plan was to travel around the country
then end up in Perth on the west coast with my aunt and
uncle, along with the rest of my relatives out there. But
as with everything else in my life, BMX got in the way.

I'd ordered a custom-made bike from the US six
months previously. It took longer than I thought and
eventually touched down at Aberdeen airport on 10
June, which was far from ideal, and I'd paid £1,000 for
it, a fair amount of cash then. That was just for the frame,
fork, bar and pegs, not the wheels or anything else.

I was down in Dundee saying goodbye to my parents
so my mate Paul Morrison did me a massive, massive
favour. He went to the airport and collected it but had
to pay £220 to clear customs – and then he drove like a
man possessed to get it to me.

I was not taking a lot, starting a new life in Australia with one single bag. So I had crammed in all the clothes I needed; mainly my FUCT t-shirts.

I got into them after seeing the singer Zack de la Rocha from Rage Against The Machine wearing them. The letters were done in the same font as the Ford logo and at a quick glance it looked the same – but then you had a closer look and saw it wasn't. I had built my collection up to about 25 or so then Paul turned up and I had to get my entire bike, including tyres, into this suitcase.

Fuck knows how I did it but finally I jammed it closed and it tipped the scales at 44kg. Excess luggage had to be paid but at least I was starting my new adventure with my bike – and my beloved t-shirts.

Sadly not all of them made it intact and I winced standing at the baggage carousel at Tullamarine airport in Melbourne as my suitcase came trundling into sight, and it was slashed open across the top. I can imagine some poor baggage handler was frustrated at the sheer weight of it – and thought, 'I'll teach this bloody joker a lesson.' And whoever he or she was, they had in the process ripped up a few of the FUCTs but the ones that made it, I've still got them – and they went on to cause a bit of a stir on national TV too over there.

I left the airport and met up with a girl I'd got to know at Alpine Bikes, Ollerenshaw. She was a mountain biker for the Cannondale brand and had told me to look her up when I arrived in Melbourne. My plan was to stay with her for two weeks then leave the city. Fuck me – I ended up staying for 18 years.

Jane took me down to the ramps and bike parks as I was gagging to get on my new bike and rip it up in the glorious sunshine.

And it was immense. This thing that I had been salivating for, I was doing it and riding topless in the warm air while loving life. What really helped me was that back then the UK and US were ahead of Australia in terms of BMX – Down Under, they didn't have our standard of competition. So when the other riders saw me doing 540 airs and all these other big tricks, they were pretty taken aback. And to top it off, I was doing them on this shit-hot, custom-made top-of-the-range Standard Byke – designed for my exact measurements – that they'd only eyed up in a catalogue. Standards were top quality machines and you didn't see them that often. So it was a case of, 'Who the fuck is this crazy Scotsman?'

That was great for me as everyone was talking to me and I struck up a rapport with a lad called Troy Brook. We got on so well that I moved in with him and he got me a job, so I didn't have to make the dreaded call to my aunt and uncle begging for cash for food. I was sanding kitchen cabinets. Just sanding. And more sanding. It was another pretty unglamorous job but I was into it, as I could knock off in the afternoon and go ride my bike.

I still didn't see BMX as a career, even at this point when I clearly had the skills and dedication to make it one. I just had so much freedom and the weather meant I could ride almost right into the night, seven days a week – with no rain, ice, snow or fog to get in the way of my practice sessions.

The nightlife was great too. I recall hitting the club Juice pretty early and they sold a 12-month entry medallion for $100 so I thought it was good value. I decided to get it, which meant I didn't have to queue and could just cut to the front of the line. With that, and my Scottish accent going down a storm with the ladies, I felt like a VIP in Melbourne and I'd only been there about a month.

Then things took a weird turn. One of the guys at work told me through the haze of the sawdust that was always around me that his wife was a cleaner for a well-known casting agent. I'm not sure why but I kind of blurted out that I'd be up for some of that.

One thing led to another and this casting agent – Liz Mullinar – got me an audition at the offices of Barry Michael Artists, who were agents for all sorts of stars. I don't know how but Liz must have taken pity on me and got me in the door, and Barry's son Aaron auditioned me.

I don't know what he made of me but the proof is in the pudding – and he signed me up. I was on his books. The only thing I needed was to get some professional head shots done. I didn't have a clue where you got them done but Aaron dispatched me to see this guy called Alan Fletcher.

It was only when I walked into the studio that I realised I knew Alan very well. He is in fact the zany doctor Karl Kennedy in *Neighbours*. He's still in the role today, even going around student unions in Britain playing to thousands of fans. Alan did the business with my snaps but I never really thought it would lead to anything until I started to get calls from my agents, telling me to go to this audition or that casting session. I ended up appearing in TV shows like *State Coroner* and *Blue Heelers*.

I was then cast in *Neighbours*, which was mega as I'd watched it back home and still remembered the excitement of meeting the Blakeney twins back in Dundee. I did three years, starting out just as an extra, to becoming a featured extra – meaning I'd get to say the occasional line.

I'd pop up in episodes all the time, doing something in the background. It was a fucking riot. *Neighbours* was huge back in the UK with each episode being screened on BBC1 at lunchtime and early evening – so with no acting skills, I'd arguably ended up in the country's biggest TV show.

It's still going today but isn't quite as popular – it really was massive and the famous wedding of Kylie Minogue and Jason Donovan was watched by 20 million people in Britain alone.

The show is set in a real suburban street but it uses the fictional name of Ramsay Street – and the set was a great place to spend my off-the-bike time. It was a lot of fun and there were plenty of stunning ladies to chat up.

I remember getting to know Holly Valance, who went on to become a big-time sex symbol and pop star. We had a race on Melbourne's South Eastern Freeway after filming one day. She was in her Honda Prelude, it was a fast bugger – and I had my Mitsubishi VRX. Who won? I think it was Holly.

The parties on *Neighbours* were legendary. The Christmas bash was the talk of the city, everyone would go nuts and plenty of debauchery went on. Anne Haddy, who has sadly passed away now having played the show's battle-axe Helen Daniels with distinction, suffered one New Year and they had to put something into the show to explain it a little.

Nothing much was really made of it though as Anne was a bit older and mobility can sometimes go. But the real story was that she got so pissed at the Christmas party she went for a booze-induced flyer and broke her hip.

I never really thought about anyone seeing me in *Neighbours* as I was just an extra, until a letter arrived from Dundee. It was from the mum of Iain Carnegie – my partner in crime at the building site. Jane wrote bluntly that she couldn't enjoy the show any more as she kept seeing me and it didn't look right.

Some viewers also noticed my subtle bit of banter as the *Neighbours* wardrobe team loved that I wore my FUCTs on screen. So as I flashed by in the background, some punters would spit out their coffee and go, 'Did that guy's shirt say fuck on it?'

The performing wasn't that demanding for me as I was used to doing it on my bike – this was even easier as there was no chance of falling off or breaking any bones.

I was making decent cash so I stopped sanding and I then ended up in a few movies. I was an extra in Jackie Chan's action film *Mr Nice Guy* and also a comedy called *The Craic*, which was about illegal immigrants in Melbourne. I actually got shafted on *The Craic* as I was supposed to have a proper line, but the producer's nephew was in town from London and he pulled rank.

I would have a go at anything though. The most bizarre had to be when I was booked for the gameshow *The Price Is Right*. One of the prizes the contestants could win was an all-expenses-paid trip to London.

No doubt about it, that was a cracking reward for doing well on the show and they wanted me to be the visual representation. So they asked for me to be a skinhead and had me wearing big chunky Dr Marten's and jeans with braces on. As they projected iconic pictures of London up on the studio screen like Tower Bridge and Trafalgar Square, I swaggered out, but I looked like a skinhead punk. The message, in my mind, was 'Come to London and get your teeth kicked out.' How that was appealing I'll never know.

As I was on the extras circuit, I discovered there was money to be made in doing voiceovers. There wasn't exactly an abundance of Scottish guys in Melbourne so I figured I could capture the market. I got the role to do the radio ad for *Trainspotting Live*, the theatre adaptation of the movie that was coming to tour across Australia. I can still remember what I said. And if you ever encounter me in the BMX world or just passing through an airport, stop me and I'll do it for you free of charge. It was, 'If you believe that the world is a sane place, that the people in charge have your best interests at heart, that all good things come to those who wait, then you belong at home watching TV; if on the other hand you suspect that beneath that sane respectable veneer lurks a psychotic hell peopled by weirdos and junkies, and you don't know whether to laugh or scream, come see it, *Trainspotting* – just buy the ticket.'

It was a really cool thing to be part of, especially as it's probably Scotland's biggest movie of recent times. It had a huge cultural impact and everyone knows all the characters. But as it's about heroin addicts, it was maybe too raw for some Australian audiences and the tour was eventually scrapped. The company went bust and I only got ten per cent of my fee.

That was the start of the end for me in the showbusiness world with the clincher being a very bitter pill to swallow and one of the biggest slaps in the face I've ever had – and as you know, I've been thrown in an electric fire by my own father.

I got the chance to do the voice for Chum Dog Food. Their brand is based around a Scottie dog and they were launching a range of puppy treats. So I was in the studio, headphones on, behind the glass – and I had to do a couple of different scenarios. One was where the wee puppy (me) encounters a big-ass Doberman sleeping.

And I went, 'Hey ugly, you're drooling, ya great big lump of shh … surely I'm off now, if you're going to bite off more than you can chew, make sure it's Chumpy.' The other one I still remember was, 'I've quite an appetite for variety, take Penny she was nice, Maria a spirited lass, och! And Bridget all woman, there's not much I haven't tried, mmmmmmm new Jumpy chunks in gravy, why helloooo.'

The guys at the studio loved it, all pissing themselves laughing as I really went for it and even my agent was saying I had really nailed it and this could be a lucrative gig.

About a week later my agent got a call back from Chum and their board of directors had said they didn't like my accent. They explained that they didn't feel it was Scottish enough. I was apoplectic.

Are you fucking kidding me? I was the most authentic voice in the whole city – maybe even the whole country. They ended up giving it to some Aussie, who put on a really cheesy voice like the pathetic Scottish accents in *Braveheart*, they've always sounded dodgy to me and to be honest I thought they were shit. So that was it, I didn't want to do that sort of stuff anymore.

And I finally saw that there was a full-time career in BMX. It hit me like a bolt from the blue, that I could make a living out of it.

Not even a call from my parents to tell me that my biological father had died knocked me out of my stride. They knew I was still digging in hard to make my name in the sport, so they immediately said they'd pay for my airfare and to book up whatever dates suited me. I took them back a little when I said, 'I won't be coming back home for the funeral.' Why fucking would I? He was never a father to me. It's crude and not nice to say, but he inseminated my mother and I was the result. That was it.

I couldn't even tell you if he was buried or cremated, but I'd be shocked if it wasn't whatever the cheapest option was. My sister Rachel then rang me to tell me about his will and that I'd been left something. I told her that they could shove it. The guy never gave me anything when he was alive, so why would he now? I wasn't going to be a hypocrite and take whatever it was. To this day, I still don't know what it was and where it ended up.

I have no interest in knowing about my biological dad or wasting time worrying about things in the past.

The best thing I did many years later was go for a therapy session – and meditated. The doctor told me to imagine myself walking through a forest and then coming to a big, still lake. And my guide would be on the other side. I looked over and it was my biological dad and as I walked over, he smiled, I smiled back – and then he just wandered off into the distance, gradually getting further and further away until I could no longer see him. I forgave him then but he was never my dad in anything but name.

I put it out of my mind pretty quickly and kept riding. I soon had something more serious on my mind as I discovered I'd fractured my skull – for the fourth time, and I nearly died.

I was in Melbourne's Camberwell Skatepark on the ramp, a place I used to enjoy riding. I did my Scott Carroll signature rock walk drop-in like I always did, where I'd spin around 270 degrees then fall backwards into the ramp blind. Unfortunately at that precise moment another guy was going for some big air on the other bowl and the bowls are joined by the spine, where I'd dropped in from. Anyway this guy came soaring up into the air and smacked me full force in the back. I went shooting forward and didn't have time to react or break my fall so I face-planted into the concrete – and that's when everything went black.

I remember sort of coming around in the back of my friend Jordan Kolb's car as he raced me to the hospital. I was slipping in and out of consciousness but I recall pulling up to a set of traffic lights where my head was hanging out the window like a dog and I caught my reflection in another car's window. Looking back at me was Quasimodo.

I blacked out again and came back around in A&E. I was lying there and this pretty nurse was tending to me, so in my deluded state I tried to chat her up. Jordan erupted with laughter as it was bloody typical of me to be laying there half-dead but thinking about lining up a date. I was wheeled in for the CT scan and I'd fractured my eye socket along with my cheekbone. Then the doctor informed me I'd also fractured my skull. But he said, 'You'll be used to that now as you've done it three times before, I see from the scans.'

What? I hadn't an inkling and never knew. Before when I got whacked or went down hard, I'd shake it off and carry on riding. That's just what you did. With my injuries, they wanted to keep me in overnight for observation in case I took a turn for the worse. I kicked up a stink and had to override the medial advice – and signed myself out.

That was because I had a date, ironically with a nurse friend of my cousin Julie. I was still so scrambled that I couldn't remember that it was Julie though. I just knew someone had set me up and I was to go round for dinner that night. Somehow I got to Julie's place and she nearly fainted when she opened the door to me. I remember her joking to maybe sit on the other side of my date so she didn't quite have to bear the mangled mess my face was in all night. I was like something out of *Phantom of the Opera*.

We had dinner and I don't know whether the painkillers made my chat sound great but the nurse ended up staying over to look after me as she was worried I'd fall asleep and never wake up. As I was still really fried and really in a state, she ended up trying to kiss me but I was in so much pain that I couldn't even stand that. So she gave me a blowjob. I don't know how or why. I've never seen the nurse since but she might have saved my life as if I'd slipped into a deep sleep, I might not have ever woken up.

Most people probably wonder why we do it. Why do we risk our bodies to pull off a jump? And it's no joke. The thing is that no matter what happens to us, we wouldn't give it any less on our next jump or trick. We crave that feeling of going for it. In BMX, it's all about commitment and determination. There's no feeling like it.

Total mental application to one single thing. Sex. Drugs. Love. Nothing replicates what it's like for us. You hear people say in a car crash that everything slows down. It's the same for us as we fly through the air; we can see that beautiful sunset like we've been studying it for hours – or we notice the kid 20 metres away looking with his mouth open, as if we were face to face.

It took me a long time to realise that's what the sport is all about.

You're in the moment. Nothing else matters. Nothing else in your mind. BMX is almost meditation. You're free of everything and there's no baggage on the bike. It's a pure thrill and challenge to pull off whatever stunt, jump or trick we're attempting – and that's why we get back on no matter the damage to our bones, or the horror stories of other riders ending up in wheelchairs.

Writing this book, I'm 45 but on a bike, I still see things from the eyes of a kid. I feel the same as I did when I was 12 when I come flying off the ramp. There's nothing in life that will ever replace how BMX makes me feel. And it's the same for all the other pro riders.

I've got an insatiable appetite for BMX and it's the reason why I've made the sport my entire life.

* * * * *

I had really ripped into life in Melbourne; I was young, free and single – and by God, I was taking full advantage of it. But the only really serious relationship I had around this time ended because of one of the most shameful acts I've ever committed in my life. I'd begun seeing this wild but gorgeous blonde chick – she was into bikers, loved AC/DC and was really full-on. I've not included her name in this book and the reason for that will become evident.

I don't know how we ever really had a relationship as we were like fire and ice – a toxic combination is another way of putting it. If we weren't kissing we were arguing, and I don't mean petty squabbles – one time she attacked me with her stilettos and was certainly looking to do some serious damage.

She had a temper on her and would fly off the handle big time, then one day completely out of the blue she announced to me that she was pregnant. My insides went up, down and all over the place – I was under no circumstances ready to be a father and we were so unstable. I didn't think about her, I only thought about myself and I managed to talk her and cajole her into agreeing to having an abortion. But my panic was so great that I didn't want to give her time and space to book an appointment – I did it.

And then I drove her there. Even though I'd lost my licence for speeding I still bundled 'my girlfriend' into the car and we went up the clinic.

Once it was all taken care of, the weight was lifted off my shoulders and I was breathing easy. Shamefully I then decided to ditch her that day. She was in a lot of discomfort plus all the emotional stress of losing an unborn child – and what did I do? Well, I dropped her off at home, marched her up the path and into her house, handed her keys to her – and I bolted out of there as I had started doing some theatre classes, and I had one that evening. What a complete tosser.

I don't think anything will remove the stain of doing that. Somehow she didn't seem to take it as hard as she should have as we were on and off for another six months but like I said, if we weren't having some rampaging shouting match then we were tearing each other's clothes off.

Then we met up at Knox Skate Park to talk things over and she told me that she had met this guy who was in the Hell's Angels, so she wanted to know what was going to happen with us. I was pretty happy to be honest as I didn't see us having any future but one thing led to another and we had sex in my car at the park – and that was the last time we ever met up.

But I was made aware that almost exactly nine months later, she gave birth to a daughter whose father is officially the biker dude. I've seen pictures of her on Facebook and when I look at her, I see two people – my sister Agnes and my own daughter, who was yet to be born at this point. So when she turns 18, I will reach out and ask if she will take a DNA test with me, so we can find out beyond any doubt.

It's not something that keeps me awake at night, but it's something I've thought about all these years. We both need to know – if I'm her dad, I want to be part of her life and she has a half-sister, so I'm sure they both would love to know each other.

But under that cloud, I decided I should make my way to Perth – four years behind schedule. Better late than never, right? I'd also got word that my grandmother was dying of cancer so I really wanted to spend some time with her – she'd come into my life late due to the adoption, so I wanted to make up for lost time.

At this time BMX was on the rise and with my skills at a good level thanks to the great Australian weather, I was offered a deal in Perth too so I snapped that up and signed up as an official rider for the distributor of Schwinn bicycles.

Basically they supplied me with bikes and branded kit and I'd be endorsing them in the parks and at contests all over Australia, but mainly in Perth for the foreseeable future. The concept was that me doing my thing might lead someone to be impressed with some of my tricks and think, 'I'll buy a Schwinn and do that too.' Schwinn were serious operators as they'd previously sold one million units of their famous Sting-Ray. Nowadays in the bike industry, we're jumping for joy with 10,000 of one model.

I'm not sure why but I decided to drive from Melbourne and did the mammoth road trip in three and a half days. It was fucking brutal; about 2,100 miles by road. On the first day I did Melbourne to Port Augusta. When I got there I was stunned to see the blackest people I've ever come across in my life – they were Aborigines but their skin was like black leather. I'll never forget it.

The following day, I was back in the saddle and made my way up to Eucla – and I was out on seriously remote roads. I was in the car for 18 hours that day and I would only stop for a pee when I had to get petrol. I hardly came across another car or person in all that time – except a cop. I saw him in the distance through the heat haze as I was blistering down the road with my foot hard on the throttle but instead of giving me a ticket, which he would have been well within his rights to do, he just rolled down his window and did a patting slow down motion with his hand – and I flew by in a blur.

The final leg of the journey saw me hit Perth via Kalgoorlie, which is basically a mining town in the middle of absolutely nowhere. I wanted to go there as at the time on Australian television the actor Michael Richards, who played Kramer in *Seinfeld*, was doing this advert for Vodafone where he called someone from there. Call me mad – but I went there just so I could recreate that, and called my mate Greig Innes, excitedly telling him, 'I'm in Kalgoorlie.'

Finally I did arrive and it was fantastic to be able to connect with my family – and hear all their stories. I'd known them a bit but they'd immigrated not long after the adoption so we hadn't spent that much time together. While I was doing that, I got busy with doing promotional work for Schwinn and what was really popular was nightclub performances.

It sounds a bit odd, but me and the other riders would go into these packed-out clubs, and do all sort of tricks up on stage. We'd have spotlights on us and there was plenty of room, so we could do all sorts of stunts – and even the odd wall ride, if space allowed. The only snag was how hot it would get as I'd be sweating like crazy, but I was being paid for people to watch what I'd normally do for free in my spare time. Then once our set was over, I felt like a rock star. Plenty of girls – and guys to be honest – would come up, and want to ask us about it all.

Meeting women wasn't a problem though as I had my old pal Gary in Perth. He used to own a snowboarding shop next door to Alpine Bikes back in Aberdeen. I got to know his family, maybe a little too well and I'm not overly proud of this. But I ended up sleeping with his cousin, then his wife's cousin, and also got close to his sister-in-law. Don't blame me – they're a gorgeous family. But now whenever he sees me, he asks me if there's anyone in his family that I haven't been with.

RIDE

At that time I also got to know the guys at Crusty Demons of Dirt, who then went on to start Nitro Circus. They were great people and I really fitted in well. The most famous of them is probably Carey Hart, who went on to marry the pop star Pink. He's actually still a friend and they contacted me to buy a BMX – but we'll get to that later on.

I remember leaving Carey and the rest of them stunned when one day I flew off a big ramp at such speed that I actually ended up on top of a single-storey roof – it was an annex of a bigger building. Then as the adrenaline was coursing through my veins, I jumped right back off again but the coming down wasn't quite as smooth and I blew my knee out. I didn't care though.

They were all looking at me with their jaws open and shouting out that I was some sort of maniac. Ever since the days at Broughty Ferry, I had always gone for things full throttle – and I still do.

The only concession I had was buying a helmet, but I never wore it. But I've got to say that I'm not the best advert for safety – none of us are. Like most BMXers I've got injuries that will be with me until the day I die. I didn't even realise the first three times I fractured my skull.

I enjoyed Perth though. I did plenty of road trips around that part of the country, I was riding a lot and there were lots of women to keep me busy. It wasn't hard as the social scene was superb and back then the city had an 8:1 ratio of men to woman.

My success rate went to my head when I spotted this gorgeous girl on the beach while I was there so I swaggered up to her, giving her all my chat, telling her I was a BMX rider and also a serious actor – when in fact, I was an extra in *Neighbours*, one step up from the tea boy. She kind of looked at me oddly as I gave her my best lines, before she politely said she had a boyfriend and I scuttled off back to Gary.

Only when I got back did he tell me that I'd been chancing my arm with Jo Beth Taylor, a household name on Australian TV who presented lots of the big 1990s primetime shows – but she'd taken a break after a rumoured porn tape scandal broke. So there she was trying to stay out of the limelight, and I must have been the only guy on the beach who didn't recognise her – what a brasser!

With that shocker I decided it was time to get back to Melbourne as I couldn't see a way forward in Perth for my career. Being a pro BMX rider and doing well in contests had its perks in a town like that, but I wanted to really make my mark – and due to a bit of good luck and timing, an opportunity arose that I couldn't turn down.

But I wasn't going back in the same manner I came. I couldn't face that drive and back in those days when security wasn't as tight, people would sell their unwanted plane tickets in the newspaper so I spotted a one-way to Melbourne. I then booked a train to transport my car back too. Thinking back on it, you wonder how there weren't more incidents on planes as I met the chap at

Perth airport. He checked in, got his boarding pass – and then gave it to me in exchange for the cash. So essentially I pretended to be him and sneaked on to the flight sheepishly.

* * * * *

The promo work and nightclub demos, plus the contests, kept me busy – and happy. But it was still an industry where you couldn't be comfortable if you stayed solely on the bike, unless you were one of the handful of superstars like Dave Mirra and Ryan Nyquist.

So my plan was to combine my riding with some behind-the-scenes work and I was put on to an opportunity at Repco Distribution, who worked with Haro and handled their bikes being sold in Australia. They had two jobs going – one for a sales agent and one for a product manager. I really wanted the product manager gig and felt it was made for me as that's where my skills lay, in understanding and being passionate about bikes. But my mate Steve Paraskevas got it over me and I got the sales job.

The first major event happened when Steve noticed I was still a Schwinn rider and he was like, 'If you're selling Haro, you need to be one too.' So I became an Australian Team Haro rider and for the first time in my life I was presented with a desk to work from. If you've ever seen the British version of *The Office*, that's what it was like. We were all in our cubicles with our phones, bike folders, pens and staplers sprawled across our desks – and the warehouse was downstairs.

I also had to ditch my rider's uniform of shorts and t-shirts as a more formal trousers and a collar was expected in the office. I'll be frank, I hated it at the start. It was a real letdown to come from riding all day in the sunshine to being chained to a desk in an air-conditioned morgue. In some ways I felt I was back behind bars like my days at Glenrosa – it had that sort of feel to it mentally.

I suffered it though as it was the only realistic way for me to become a bigger figure in the BMX world as the pro contests paid, but not enough to have a lavish lifestyle. So I slurped it up and got on with it.

But it wasn't long before the boss gave me a ticking off. The issue was that Steve, who was in the office across from my desk, would be planning new Haro bikes – what they were going to look like, what colours they would be in and all that stuff. And he knew I was the only real rider in the office so he'd ask my opinion and I would jump right in. It got me fired up. I revelled in that kind of thing and I didn't want to be calling shops trying to sell them bikes, but my boss didn't care though. He came down on me hard and reminded me what my job title was. I tried to complain and explain I was wasted doing what I was – but I've never lacked determination so I cracked on.

I did a lot of growing up in my spell there as I'd never been a part of that sort of environment and I learned how the corporate world worked, while I was also still womanising in a big way and at the time I just thought it was my nature. Looking back I think it was because I didn't find it that challenging, I wasn't out of my comfort zone. So I reckon I chased anything with a skirt on because I wanted some sort of challenge.

One thing I did have was a lot of contacts from being a rider so I wasn't your average sales agent. I lasted two and a half years but it was getting me down and while it broke my heart to leave Haro behind, I made a move.

But I have to open up about my favourite day at work there as it's also one of my best memories of all time. Dave Mirra and Ryan Nyquist came to Melbourne as they were the Haro star riders and at this point. Dave was absolutely box office, he had a Sony Playstation game in his name and kids looked up to him all over the world. We'd met each other before at the King Of Concrete back in 1993, the year after I broke my knees, when he stayed in the same apartment as the Scottish pro rider Dave Frame and I – and it was great to be able to spend some time together again. Dave and Ryan did promotional things around Melbourne to boost Haro's name and sell more bikes and then in the evenings, we'd take them out.

One night we ended up in a bar called Frostbites where they served these sort of alcoholic slush things. We'd had a few and carried on to a strip club. I've always been pretty confident around women so I was doing my usual and chatting up the girls. And somehow I got on to telling Dave, 'If you don't touch them, it's not cheating.' He erupted with laughter when I told him that and then promptly asked for a private dance, and I'll always remember his American accent imitating my words to one of the strippers. I still laugh like a drain when I think about this all-time BMX superstar sitting there saying that. Sadly Dave took his own life in 2016 – RIP my friend.

With all this going on, I was relishing life in Australia so I decided to become a citizen. It seemed the sensible move as I adored the climate, I could ride my bike 365 days a year and I was having a ball. So I did it on 26 January 2002, which is Australia Day, and it's common for people to get their citizenship as sort of a tradition.

But I wasn't turning my back on Scotland as it's the land of my birth and will be with me forever. So as a nod to that I had a tattoo done of Scotland running from along the top of my back. It was my way of showing that whatever I do and wherever I end up, I'll always carry my country proudly on my shoulders. But it was nice to be accepted into my new home and I've still got my two passports.

And now that I'd established myself in Australia, I really wanted to put my sordid past behind me once and for all. So I flew back to Scotland aged 30 and it was time to get my shit in order. I wanted to deal with things that were still troubling, mainly in how I couldn't be faithful to a woman as I seem to have some inbuilt fear that they'd leave me, even if it was totally irrational.

My parents had left Dundee and bought a B&B in Carnoustie, a small, quaint town best known for its world-famous golf course. I wanted them to know everything I'd been through and why I'd done things to them in the past like the racism, the stealing, the disrespect and the disruption. I showed them the scars from my dad's beatings and their reaction mystified me as this was all new information. While we'd never discussed it a lot, I always thought they knew some things. They told me that they'd been informed that I was malnourished and that had been the reason for all my problems, so they didn't know any of the other stuff.

My dad took it the hardest. Poor Eldridge Buultjens, this fucking respected scientist was crying his eyes out in the dining room. He started apologising and again, he never failed to amaze. He was saying sorry for being hard on me, particularly with my school work. I nearly broke down, to see this amazing man, showing me once again how much he loved me, in such a state. I assured him and my mother, the way they'd treated me was perfect, I'd needed a kick in the balls to set me straight. I needed the example they set as it's the reason I became the man I did. Without them I'd have done nothing with my life – I had no role models until they adopted me.

The other thing on my agenda was to lock away my demons once and for all, so that meant sitting down and having it out with my biological mother. I called my sister Rachel – she was almost inseparable from my birth mum, they saw each other every single day – and asked her to meet me at Glasgow's Buchanan Street bus station. It's the major one in the city centre but she wasn't keen, and blabbered on about not liking coming into the town as it's so busy. I told her I'd flown halfway around the world to deal with my problems and see her and the least she could do is come down and meet me, then take me up to my mother's place.

By this point my mum had remarried a local guy called Eddie – they'd tied the knot in 1987. Finally Rachel saw sense and we met, then we jumped on a bus out to Drumchapel. I told her why I wanted to see my birth mother but Rachel started saying it wasn't a good idea and it might upset her. Honestly, my sister tests my patience like no one else as either she's sticking up for my biological father and offering excuses or doing things like that on the bus, trying to pretend nothing had happened and we were this happy-go-lucky family.

But I forced the issue and got one to one with my birth mother. I simply said to her, 'Mum, I forgive you.' The significance hit me as the words left my mouth as it was the first time I'd called her mum and acknowledged her as that – but she didn't seem to know what I meant and I continued, 'I forgive you for giving me away, I know it was for my own protection. I resented you for a while because of it, but I forgive you and understand.'

She ended up in tears as we talked about the past and some of the horrific things she went through. It was stomach-churning and I didn't want to hear it but I'm glad I did. It just reaffirmed that it was as bad as I'd remembered it and that was really the last time I spoke to my biological mum.

We saw each other briefly in 2012, but then she died in 2015 after having suffered from dementia and emphysema – and I never went to her funeral either, as I had already said my goodbyes and made my peace with her. We were blood but we were never close and I'd moved on.

I'm glad she did find happiness though with Eddie – they both loved to go country line dancing and were fucking chainsmokers; going into their house that day was like facing the police riot squad's tear gas canisters. They both died within a week of each other, which was a lovely thing as miraculously they'd been living apart for a few years as she was in an old folks' home and he was still living in their flat in Drumchapel. So while her passing didn't really impact upon me as I'd dealt with everything during that chat we had, it did make me smile to know that she'd died a lot happier than she'd lived as a young mother.

Feeling a lot better about things and happy that I'd dealt with a lot of the issues that had plagued me, I flew back to Melbourne eager to press on.

# 8

# Ron Jeremy

AGAIN through the community, I'd been given a nudge about another good company making their mark, Trick Bits, who distributed Mat Hoffman's range of bikes. Mat is now a good pal of mine but in those days he was merely a guy I'd marvelled at in magazines and looked up to massively. He had the reputation in BMX as the master of the tricks who would think up and create all these crazy jumps.

Mat and Dave Mirra were the two main guys who did all the big jumps and tricks but while most of us BMX fanatics saw Mat as the one who created them, Dave perfected them.

He would see what Mat did and then make it work for a mainstream audience – and that's how he ended up with Sony PlayStation games in his name.

Anyway, it was the lure of this sort of connection that made me switch. I've always massively respected

Mat and the way he threw himself at jumps was hugely inspiring – he's the BMX idol, for the real BMX kids. He's been clinically dead twice due to going for it without a single second of hesitation and to be selling his brand was something I didn't have to think twice about.

Even better, I could go back to being the BMX kid I'd always been, so the smart trousers and shirts with a collar were tossed in the bin – and I was back in my trusty shorts and t-shirts.

A lot of people might think that is unprofessional and not appropriate for doing business. But I disagree. Does a bike shop owner want a guy looking all prim and proper, who knows his figures but nothing about BMX? Or does he want me? I know everything there is to know as I actually ride the bikes and do the jumps. I am totally professional and in my profession, you wear shorts and a t-shirt. No one does flying air jumps in a Hugo Boss suit in the same way David Beckham didn't go out on the pitch in designer jeans; it's a mindset.

I jumped at the chance to be back where I felt comfortable. When I was trying to sell Haro I'd really just take the bikes to the shops and use my passion to convey what they were all about.

I didn't have to fake it, as from the day I saw *ET* I'd been a Haro junkie. I was that BMX kid standing in the shop eyeing up the gleaming new bikes, it was no act.

And with Hoffman I was back to being that on a day-to-day basis. I'd ask the buyers to come to the local skatepark or ramp and I'd show them right there what the bikes were all about.

I always felt, and still feel, that the bikes sell themselves if you show what they're capable of and how much freedom they give you. The even sweeter angle to the new job was they wanted me. So I bagged an increase in salary, and I was also given a car and a fuel allowance – as Australia is a bloody big country. While I was based in Melbourne, I was going all over the place to sell bikes. I wasn't pushy or trying to ram things down people's throats and I had a golden rule that I still abide by now – I won't endorse or sell any bike that I wouldn't ride myself.

Hoffman was a load of fun and I had a new bike sponsor. Of course, I had to switch over to riding their bikes too and one day during filming of a show session for them, I met my wife Samantha as she walked past Camberwell Skatepark – my horrendous accident previous hadn't put me off the place. We were doing some stuff to camera for a TV show on Channel V. It was me and a young Stevie McCann, who's since gone on to win numerous gold medals at the X Games – we've been tight since I met him when he was only 11.

Anyway, I was on the ramp and I don't know why but I just sensed this woman's presence in the vicinity behind me. I looked over and saw Sam so I immediately dropped my bike and sprinted to the fence, vaulted it and chased after this bemused girl. She began speed-walking to escape me; this man who, in her eyes, was a deranged idiot pursuing her. But I caught up with her and we walked down to the junction of Riversdale Road.

I was really out of breath, but I said how great she looked and that I'd love to take her out. She snapped back, 'What are you doing playing with those kids?' I was like, 'Nah, nah, I'm a pro rider.' Anyway I didn't want to hassle her, so I gave her my business card and left, I really didn't want to be the asshole calling her up and bugging her to come out on a date. So I thought that if I left my number, the ball would be firmly in her court.

Leaving it at that, I ran back, jumped over the fence and got ready to start filming again but the director was grinning widely and marvelling at what he'd seen me do. He was telling me it was the best pick-up he'd ever seen and somehow, he saw something in me that sparked an idea in his imagination.

Because of that, he offered me a job interviewing Ron Jeremy in a few weeks. I didn't know who Ron was but Stevie jumped in, informing me that he was the biggest porn star on the planet. I've never turned down a challenge so I told the director to count me in but I put that to the back of my mind as I had bigger fish to fry, as the following day I was off to Adelaide for work.

And while I was there, the girl I had accosted on the street called. She told me her full name was Samantha Connor and we chatted away. I didn't know it yet but she would change my life forever.

I wasn't surprised she called as I felt there was this connection, even though I didn't know her. Once I got

Extract of an entry from the REGISTER OF BIRTHS in Scotland    6933519 CE

| BIRTH | District No. 611 | Year *1972* | Entry No. *264* | N.H.S. No. | 6 | 1 | 1 | 7 | 2 | 2 | 6 | 4 |

REGISTERED IN THE DISTRICT OF  GLASGOW

1. Surname **Craig**

Name(s) **John Jackson**

2. Sex **m**

3. When born 19.72. **March Sixteenth** 2330 hours

4. Where born **Queen Mothers Hospital, Glasgow**

5. Mother's name(s) and surname **Margaret Atkinson Craig**

6. Maiden surname **Gardner**

7. Mother's usual residence (if different from 4 above) **7 Glendore Street. Glasgow**

8. Father's name(s) and surname **Thomas Jackson Craig.**

9. Occupation **Engineer's Labourer**

10. Date and place of parents' marriage — Year **1966** Month **3** Day **7** Place **Glasgow**

11. Informant's signature and qualification **Thomas Craig Father**

12. When registered — Year **1972.** Month **3** Day **20**

13. **J. Galbraith** Registrar

14.

*Adopted*

This official document is issued by the General Register Office for Scotland, New Register House, 3 West Register Street, Edinburgh EH1 3YT under the Seal of that Office on  **03 December 2014.**

The above particulars incorporate any subsequent corrections or amendments made with the authority of the Registrar General.

**Warning**

It is an offence for any person to pass as genuine any copy or reproduction of an extract issued from the General Register Office for Scotland if it has not been authenticated by the Seal of that Office.

Any person who falsifies or forges any of the particulars on this extract or knowingly uses, gives or sends as genuine any false or forged extract is liable to prosecution.

This extract is evidence of an event recorded in the registers held by the General Register Office for Scotland; it is NOT evidence of the identity of the person presenting it.

*My original birth certificate as John Craig but it wasn't a name I'd use for long, 1972*

*Here's me at
five years old,
1977*

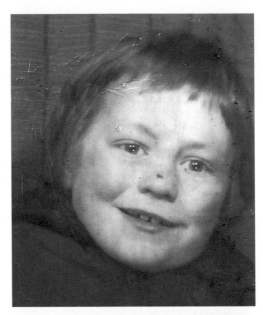

*Me and my birth father
Thomas look happy, but
we never were, 1981*

*Marianna and Eldridge write to me and Agnes, 1982*

Dear John and Agnes,
We are called:
Eldridge and Marianna.
This is a picture of us
taken on Christmas Day.
We were thinking of you.

*Next to Marianna and Eldridge's Nissan, the first car I'd been in that didn't belong to the cops or the social services, 1983*

*After the
adoption,
me and my
wee sister
at Dunard
Primary
School, 1983*

*This time the happiness was for real, me and my new dad in
Edinburgh, 1984*

*All of us at the family home in Dundee back in 1986*

*The ramp at Broughty Ferry. It doesn't look much but it's where it all began for me, 1988*

*The ramp I built with my mate Iain. The wood was all stolen, 1987*

*Showing off my burgeoning skills on our garden wall at Roxburgh Terrace in Dundee, 1988*

*Making my TV debut after a trick gone wrong with Jeremy Beadle on* You've Been Framed, *1991*

*Pulling off a Miami Hopper in 1989*

*Topping up my BMX-induced six-pack, which some local girls admitted to me later in life was the main reason they watched me doing jumps, 1992*

The invitation to my 21st, designed by future Snow Patrol star Tom Simpson, 1993

In my chef's whites at The Angus Thistle Hotel, 1992

A broken ankle due to a wild trip to England, 1992

*Riding up a wall, I've always loved doing it, 1992*

*My business card in Australia where I got into the professional BMX business, 2002*

**John Buultjens**
Mb: 0407 665 510
Ph: (03) 9704 5300
Fax: (03) 9704 5800

*The only picture that exists of me and my three siblings Thomas, Agnes and Rachel, 2002*

*A lovely memento of a bewildering few hours in the company of porn king Ron Jeremy, 2002*

*Me and the BMX boys on the Jim Bean-sponsored Planet X trip to New Zealand, 2002*

*My proudest moment in life, holding my baby girl Mackenzie Mae – but still sporting a BMX shirt, 18 January 2007*

*I had to include a BMX even in my big day, as I married Samantha, 31 December 2005*

*Me and billionaire Forest Lucas, who put up the cash to make my life into a movie, 2016*

---

**HARODESIGN**

To Whom in May Concern:

I would like to offer this letter of recommendation for John Buultjens regarding his attempt to accept the position of BMX Brand Manager at Haro Bicycles. I founded Haro Bicycles in 1978 and in 1982 I invented the first Freestyle specific frame and fork that allowed the emerging sport to grow to the largest single category in 20" BMX today. As you probably know, Haro Bicycles is a leader in the specialty segment and it was the foundation I built and the legacy I left behind that has allowed its continued success.

Although I left the business in the early 90's to start several other businesses my name is forever attached to the brand where ever I go and as such it's my hope and concern that the care and feeding of the brand continue so that what I built remains for another 30 years and reflects positively on my name and my current business endeavors. In this spirit, I offer up this letter of recommendation and I do so with great confidence. John Buultjens was known to me long before the job position opened up at Haro. The 80's were a magical time in the sport of BMX and Freestyle specifically. There are people who have studied this period of time and have become significant collectors of Haro products in the very same way one would collect automobiles. In fact they become so engaged that they seem to know more about me, where I was, what I did, when I did it etc than I do. John is such a person, and is known to own the world's largest and most complete collection of the Haro bikes I designed during the period valued well in excess of $100,000.

Being around for another 30 years however depends on your next step and Johns most recent experience with Pilgrim Bikes in Australia gives him the unique ability to not only know the history of the brand intimately but also to navigate the future strategically ensuring continued stability and growth not only for the brand but its 25 plus California based employees. I believe that John has great character and would be a great asset not only to Haro Bicycles but to the current citizens of the United States as well. Should you have any questions please don't hesitate to contact me.

Sincerely,

BOB HARO.

Bob Haro
President/CEO BHIkonix

*The letter from Bob Haro that helped get me into the US, 2012*

*The movie cast all together. I'm on the right hand side, 2016*

*Emmy winner Bryan Craig and I on the set. I think he's going to be a big name, and we even suspect we're related, 2016*

*Rapper and movie star Chris 'Ludacris' Bridges looking dapper as my dad as we shoot in California, 2016*

*I could get used to this Hollywood life. Here's me with two talented females, Sasha Alexander and Jessica Serfaty, 2016*

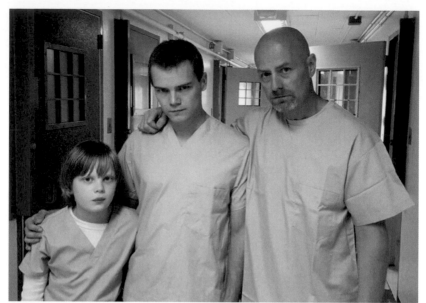

*Surreal – me in triple! Alexander Davis who plays me as a boy, Shane Graham who is me as a young man and then some old guy from Glasgow, 2016*

*Proving I've still got plenty left in the tank as I tear up a ramp in San Diego earlier this year, 2017*

back I picked her up and we went for some pasta near her place. I think she was still a bit wary of me though as she didn't let on which apartment was hers and just gave me the number of the entrance to the building.

We had a great night and then had another date that same week and got to that awkward moment where when dropping her off, she asked if I wanted to come in. I refused, which was very out of character for me, but I just felt Samantha was different so we spent ages kissing in my car instead. I told her that I wouldn't sleep with her until I'd known her for three months. I knew if we ended up in bed before that I ran the risk of ruining it and it ending up like the rest of my relationships – which all imploded after not too long.

While all this was going on, there was a Planet X event in New Zealand which I was part of – it was their version of the X Games. I had been made sports director, which basically meant being in charge of all the BMX boys. God knows why the hell they picked me as I was not responsible. I think the one thing I had over the other guys was that I had a good grasp of numbers and business. I had a budget of $100,000 for each of the 70 athletes going and the flight was on a Thursday afternoon and of course as luck would have it, the TV guy got back in touch to tell me the Ron Jeremy interview was happening the same day, in the morning. I still went for it.

It was at SEXPO, which is an annual sexuality and lifestyle exhibition in Melbourne. I got down there and was given my media pass at the accreditation desk – and in I went like an official member of the media. The director took me aside and informed me that Ron was majorly in demand, so was only doing five one-on-ones – and I was getting one of those slots. He said we had a strict 120-second time limit so I had to work it and get something good to use for the broadcast. I had no idea or plan what I was going to talk about. I was into women and partying, but I'm not a big fan of porn and haven't seen any of Ron's exploits on camera.

I was third to go and when I got ushered in, I just introduced myself and off we went. He asked me what I did and I was just upfront; there was no point pretending I was a real reporter. So I told him, 'I'm really a BMX pro who's ended up getting this gig after jumping over a fence to talk to a girl.' And as soon as he heard BMX, his ears pricked up and he started telling me how he loved it and even sponsored a few riders back in the US, like Tim Fuzzy Hall and Carey Hart, through one of his companies.

We got right into it and I kid you not, 20 minutes later we were still going. His media handlers were looking a bit nervous but Ron didn't give a shit. I also asked him something that I'd always wanted to know about. I wondered if he reckoned I could ever do porn, even though my willy wasn't that big. He told me, it's not about your size, it's about how much you cum.

Eventually we had to wrap up as he got told there were 200 proper reporters waiting outside in the hall for his press conference but Ron didn't want to stop chatting, so he told me to walk with him, and just before he went in to talk to the journalists he asked me if he could sign a DVD for me. I mean, he was asking me. What a fucking legend.

So he signed it 'To Scottish John' and we had a quick handshake and he disappeared into a flurry of camera flashes, as I just walked out of the building on my own and jumped in my car. I drove over to Stevie's house – and then we made a beeline for the airport. It was only on the plane to New Zealand that I sort of exhaled and thought, that was pretty damn cool.

We were heading for Auckland and it was a pretty wild trip. You had all these extreme riders, plenty of money and Jim Beam sponsoring the whole thing. During the day the contests were on the go but at night, we'd be partying. I also got to meet up again with Carey Hart, we'd been introduced at Planet X years before, and we had a wee chat at the event, but at the party I'd stayed clear of him. It was nothing personal but the motocross guys have this tradition of ripping the sleeves of your t-shirt. It's a sort of ritual and if you're around them, it's the done thing, but I like my t-shirts and I've still got a lot of my beloved FUCTs so I made sure I kept my distance. I didn't want to be the guy who had to say to Carey as he was mid-rip, 'Do you mind not doing that, pal?'

On the final night there we were at a mega bash and of course, free Jim Beam was all over the place as in those days you could be sponsored by a drinks company like that – nowadays alcohol is not allowed so energy drinks have taken its place.

Anyway, I was setting up all the boys and like I've said, I never lacked a brass neck or guts. So I was happily chatting away, introducing the riders to some of the females but I was staying clear as I had Samantha in mind. I really felt something special was going to happen with her but I got fucking hammered and I ended up so out of my tree that this busty redhead, Leanne Wylie, caught my eye.

We're still friends on Facebook, if it helps in my defence.

I marched over to her and said, 'I want to lick your teeth.' A lot of women would have been repulsed by a drunk Scotsman right up in their face saying that but she pouted her lips and smiled, showing off her gnashers. And I licked them. I've never asked a woman that before or since, but we ended up in bed that night.

The next day on the flight back to Melbourne, I was racked with guilt. I was sitting next to Stevie telling him how I'd fucked up big time. He told me to calm down as me and Samantha weren't really a couple yet as it had only been a few weeks. But I had never been big on commitment and was always cheating on my partners, I put it around plenty to say the least, and as I sank back in my seat I just hoped my daft night of fun wouldn't come back to bite me on the arse.

\* \* \* \* \*

While I'd been happy at Trick Bits, a few things started to happen that didn't sit well with me and I began hearing rumours that a few bills weren't being paid. They started to get stronger and then the bikes weren't coming in on time so it was a gradual thing and it culminated when the top brands started to sign with other distributors. The problem was I was still employed by them, so instead of waking up passionate I started to feel like it was a chore.

One of the new brands that we got to take up the slack was Rock Machine, which to me is complete and utter shit. There was no way I could sell that and didn't want to. It's not about street cred or appearing exclusive; my mantra has always been the bike must be designed with care, love and be able to handle what a rider puts it through, whether that's a wee kid from Glasgow or someone like Robbie Maddison jumping the Arc De Triomphe in Las Vegas.

Thankfully, because I was popular and had a good name, rising company Triplesix wanted me and it was a perfect fit for me, as it was 100 per cent BMX bikes only and they had some kick-ass brands like We The People which is top-class, as well as The Shadow Conspiracy. Another BMX pal of mine, Clint Millar, a legend from the 1990s in the sport, recommended me.

So the bosses flew me out to Sydney for a meeting where we talked shop, strategy and all that kind of thing. It was a great match and they wanted me – and I fancied the change but they had to admit that I was out of their price range. They couldn't afford to pay me what I was worth as their company was still on the way up, but not there yet. Thinking on my feet and keen to get back working with brands I wanted to be associated with, I said, 'Okay look, forget a salary, give me ten per cent of what I make you.' They thought I was mad and didn't take long to shake my hand.

So I was back on my grind and within my first three months there, I'd made them $250,000 on my own – they were pleased and I was too. By the end of that first year, I got my sales up to around $500,000 and the reason I could do that basically on my own was down to my reputation.

The shops across Australia knew two things; I didn't endorse shit and I would stay true to my word. I wasn't interested in landing a one-off deal that loaded them up with a pile of junk. I wanted the kids on the best BMX bikes possible. It might sound corny but it mattered to me, to cruise by a skatepark and see the boys or girls riding the best equipment they could afford.

Basically it kept going so well that I was flying and we got into some pretty big numbers, and at that point the ten per cent wasn't really representative of what I was doing. I was making them serious cash so we came to a deal that my apartment was registered as a Melbourne office, which meant I lived rent-free. A company car and a mobile phone soon followed too as the bosses recognised I'd been a valuable addition so I had no overheads, and all my commission left me plenty to live on.

Life was sweet and things were moving with Samantha too as we had become a proper couple and were living together – but of course, before we slept together she did ask me about the three-month rule I'd imposed right at the beginning of our relationship. She wanted to know if I had been with anyone else during that period and my heart sank so I came clean on my Jim Beam-infused night over in New Zealand. It wasn't cheating and I stand by that, as we weren't a couple and I only ever said I wouldn't sleep with her for three months. Well, that was my excuse anyway so I hadn't broken my word but still, it wasn't the best beginning to our relationship. But she understood where I was coming from.

We moved in together and I was happy as Larry. I had the girl, the job and was still living my dream of being able to ride in the glorious sunshine every day. While it might sound like I'd grown up and I had to some extent, as I was now making sure the gas and electricity bills were paid, I was still that BMX kid. This period of my life was probably the most stable in terms of my day to day. I worked hard, riding away and also building a life with Samantha, so much so that I'd left my bachelor pad and we'd bought a house together in Wantirna South, in the suburbs of Melbourne. It was also the first actual property I owned and I didn't do too badly, as it had an eight-foot-deep swimming pool, which was something I'd always wanted. I felt pretty damn happy with myself.

Marriage was then discussed, and we both felt it was a step we wanted to take but nothing was set in stone although we did pop into the Australian Diamond Company in Melbourne. They don't sell rings but just the stones.

It's one of those places where you get buzzed in through a steel door. Samantha took a shine to the Princess Cut diamonds but didn't buy anything as we wanted to look elsewhere, but I'd made a mental note of what I would be back for.

Unbeknownst to her, I returned and snapped up a 0.75 carat Princess Cut as I'd come up with this plan to get it set in a ring. I don't know anything about jewellery but I managed to get it set with 18 small diamonds underneath it – it's known as an invisible setting. Now I had the sparkler, all I needed was her dad's agreement as I wanted to do it the old-fashioned way. We were in his car on the way to Samantha's brother's place for a family gathering and I asked Terry – Sam's dad – if I could have his daughter's hand in marriage. He just looked over and said, 'It's not up to me.' Bloody hell, I knew that but I was hoping at least to get his blessing, so that was a bit of an anti-climax.

Anyway I was derailed and waited it out until later that year we flew back to Dundee for my wee sister Agnes's wedding to Bobby. That night, after they'd sealed the deal, I thought it was the perfect chance to ask Samantha officially to be my wife. I was there in my kilt, she was in the bathroom freshening up for bed, so I scanned the room trying to think of what was the right way to pop the question.

I've not held much back in this book, but I'll have to leave this little bit to the imagination. I couldn't face my parents again if they knew the ins and outs but let's just say we were doing what young couples do and making love when I asked her. I wouldn't call it the most romantic proposal but she said yes on the spot. My parents were over the moon as they'd gone from having no kids married off to having both of us practically wed in the space of a few hours.

We flew back to Australia in fine fettle but there was no real plan on when we'd do it. But then I just felt 'let's get it done' and I wanted to go for 1 January 2006 as there's no way I would ever forget that anniversary. Samantha was also happy to get up the aisle and we settled on 31 December.

It was a small affair in her parents' back yard, which was right on the beach overlooking the ocean. It was a dream setting and sadly my parents didn't make it due to short notice. I really wanted them to be there but I felt it was a lot of money to shell out and I told them not to worry. My best man was my close friend Paul Robertson, whom I have known since my days visiting Aberdeen in the late 1980s, and as luck would have it he was living then in Melbourne. My cousin Julie and her family from Glasgow were there so I felt some family presence for sure.

That felt right, as if the stars had aligned, and after we'd tied the knot we went on to this old winery nearby.

It was out of a postcard with all this rustic farming equipment giving it a real charm. As Samantha is an introvert, the polar opposite of me, we just had a few close friends and some family there. Saying that, it was the perfect way to end the year and the perfect way to begin a new one – as a married couple and a new beginning.

I'd come from nothing and there I was with a gorgeous wife, a lovely place where I could stick on my shorts and go for a swim in my back garden whenever I wanted – and those midnight dips together were magic times, especially on balmy summer nights.

Little did I know, my rollercoaster life was set to hit some stony ground, and most of it would be my fault.

# 9

# Mackenzie Mae

BEING married was great fun for me at the start and we had our home in Wantirna South, so things were going great. And as most newly married couples plan on, we also got the fantastic news that we would be becoming three as Samantha was pregnant. I was over the moon and she was stoked. It seemed like everything was coming together perfectly. I was still the BMX kid but now I was about to become – and more importantly – ready to be, a father.

I was still entering contests, riding as much as I could, and I was working for Triplesix so I was earning enough cash to keep the party going. But tragedy struck when Samantha had a miscarriage.

We had gone for the check-up scans and there was no movement. It was simple and blunt – we'd lost our baby. Sam didn't take the news well. She broke down and just couldn't understand why this had happened – we'd been so careful and done everything you're supposed to. Her parents Maria and Terry drove over to comfort us on what was the worst day of our lives. We were hit for six and it's not easy picking up the pieces from something like that.

We did it, but the cracks that it caused were in some ways the beginning of the end for the domestic bliss we'd both been enjoying. Later in the year Samantha managed to get pregnant again so it was game on again and this time we were extra, extra careful. We were back getting ready once again for the pitter-patter of tiny feet.

I'm not the most cautious guy on the planet but even I felt we had to take any pressure off our shoulders so we decided it would be smart to sell up, make a profit, bank the cash – and move back into my old place, the one that Triplesix were paying for. That way we could save some money and then move into a proper family home once the baby arrived. It used to be just my place before Samantha was on the scene but I wanted it to not feel like that. Kind of like your wife moving into your bachelor pad, there's something not quite right in that, and picking up the discarded bras and the odd earring down the back of the sofa and that sort of thing wasn't going to be a good look.

Financially I've always tried to live within my means, not beyond them, and we had money at hand so we splashed out on some new furniture. I like things bespoke, I've got that particular streak in me. It's not about something being expensive but I like my stuff to have that little touch of class and stand out. So I went and saw my friend Jarred Dowson's dad and ordered a bed, tall boy and drawers made of solid teak from old church pews from south-east Asia, which all in cost about $10,000 and I had to get them shipped over to Melbourne. When everything turned up it looked great and I was glad I went to that effort rather than going down to Ikea and getting it all done in an afternoon. So there we were, settling into our 'new' place and Samantha hit me with a massive curveball.

I never saw it coming but she told me that we would not be having sex until after the baby was born as she was worried, and correctly so, of miscarrying again. I've always enjoyed being with females, that's pretty obvious, but I realised the bigger picture and fell into line as it felt good to be a part of a serious married couple.

Down the line, we were enjoying a day at Sam's parents' place and suddenly she began bleeding. Panicked, we clambered into the car and rushed to the hospital in Geelong, which was 30 minutes' drive, just to make sure everything was okay, but by the time we got there the bleeding had increased and became heavy. I felt helpless. Thankfully our health insurance was good so they gave Sam a private room – it even had her own bathroom, plus a sofa for me to sleep on. The doctors put Sam on a drip, urging her to rest as I watched her finally fall asleep – and I wasn't long behind her.

The next day, me and Sam's parents were all stumbling about the corridors like zombies as we tried not to think of another miscarriage happening. But the doctor appeared and reassured me that Sam was doing fine – as was the baby – and told me to go home to rest. I left around about 10pm and drove home feeling as good as anyone could, given the situation. I remember my head barely touching the pillow when the phone rang. It was Sam: 'I'm in labour, the baby is coming.' I went, 'Yeah, sure she is,' and fell back asleep only for the phone to spring into life again, but this time it was the midwife, 'John, you'd better get here as your wife and child are in trouble.'

I looked at the clock. It was 4.40am. I raced out to the car and broke the speed limit the whole way back to hospital. When I arrived but they wouldn't let me in with Sam already as her mother was in there and they wouldn't allow a second person in, but all the frustration and emotion of the previous few days built up and I screamed, 'I'm the father.'

Finally they gave me a gown and I got in to see Sam having an emergency caesarean, which ended with Mackenzie Mae Buultjens arriving on 18 January at 5.30am – she was four weeks premature but who gave a shit about that.

Even BMX was part of that day as I was wearing one of my DIG t-shirts while I held my daughter for the first time, on the proudest day of my life. I could scarcely believe this little bundle of joy was a part of me and all of my complicated upbringing and the twists and turns had led to this wee girl arriving.

We chose Mackenzie as a name, not only as a nod to my Scottish heritage but also when Samantha was a child her favourite doll was called that and she'd always wanted that name for her first child since then. Mackenzie had to stay in an incubator for a few weeks due to her size but she grew very quickly while Sam stayed in hospital for the week too to recover. It was difficult for us to go home and leave Mack, but we knew she was in good hands with the excellent team of doctors and nurses.

A few weeks had gone by and it was finally time for her to come home, and what a thrill it was to bring her through the door for the first time. This wrapped-up, warm little package was ours. I took – and still do – being a dad seriously as Eldridge is a wonderful father. I wanted to be just like him and I've seen the other side of it from my biological father, so I knew how I wanted to go about it and I was determined to raise Mackenzie Mae the right way.

\* \* \* \* \*

Personally things were flying, but they were coming apart at Triplesix. I'd really got into my groove, maybe it was the pressure of having to feed another mouth or just maturity, but I was handling business. I'd managed to start bringing in revenue of around $1.8m, pretty serious numbers considering where the company started and where it was when they asked me to join – but they started messing me about.

The company agreed that ten per cent had become a six-figure sum and they didn't want to or couldn't give it to me in cash. I noticed this and tried to think through what to do but eventually I hit boiling point and called a meeting. I explained to the owners what the issue was and they gave me wishy-washy stuff on the business growing, so overheads and more staff were needed, but that wasn't my problem. We had a simple deal but as a way of breaking the deadlock, the idea of me launching my own range of bikes was mooted. It was the natural step for me as I'd earned my stripes riding and I had the reputation, I knew how to sell them, so it was the next thing to do.

We verbally agreed on a 50-50 split between them and me and the range was going to be called Forgotten. They flew down to do all the paperwork and we met at a conference room in Melbourne's Hyatt. I strode in and I was just about keeping my lid on the shortfall in my ten per cent earnings but by God, I blew my top when I saw the contract for Forgotten as after we'd spoken on the phone, something had gone on but the proposed set-up was 75 per cent to them, with me getting a 25 per cent share.

Fucking hell. I tore into them and really let them have it and told them it was total bullshit and not acceptable. I got so worked up that I took the keys to the Melbourne house and the company car, throwing them across the table. I had the savings to get Samantha and Mackenzie out of there so I was serious. I'm big on integrity and it's why I only sell or endorse products that I would ride or use.

They were taken aback and clearly thought that I would not react in that way, but they didn't fight fire with fire as they weren't stupid. They wanted to make cash and realised I was helping them trouser millions of dollars, so they said, 'Can you give us ten minutes?' I went for a walk around the block, let them have a quick pow-wow and came back, but I left the keys on the table as I wanted them to know this was no bluff.

After getting a breath of air, I'd cleared my mind but I was still furious but they had a new proposal for me. They weren't moving on the split but to sweeten things, they offered me a six-figure salary guaranteed, a quarter of the new company and said I could continue working on the selling side outside of that. Inside, I knew it was a yes as very few BMX riders were getting those sorts of guaranteed sums, outside of riding. And here was me, with a dreadful academic record and only a hotel diploma to my name, being handed serious cash. I knew I could market and sell the bikes so I was going to be earning way over my $100,000 retainer.

This was 2007 so the world economy was set to enter meltdown, but my bank balance was looking up. I played it cool and pretended to think it over, but I wasn't going to turn this deal down as it had a good mix of guaranteed cash and incentive share to give me that drive. I took back the keys to the house and car, then signed the deal.

As I walked out, I grabbed my phone and rang Samantha, laying out the broad strokes and told her to go find some land so we could build our dream family home down on the coast. Where we were living was more built-up and she wanted to go back to near her parents, who live at Ocean Grove, south of Geelong. It's the stereotypical Aussie beach town; nearby is Bell's Beach which is where the massive brands Quicksilver, Rip Curl and Billabong were all formed. It's idyllic with gorgeous sand, sunshine all year and a nice sea breeze. It's also where they filmed the original *Point Break* movie with Keanu Reeves.

So a few weeks later Samantha set off to scour the area as I had to fly to Las Vegas. It was my first trip to Sin City, host to Interbike – the largest bike show in North America – every year at the Mandalay Bay Convention Center. It's one of the largest shows in the world and everyone comes from near and far to show off their new models and build up a buzz. I was off with Forgotten but we were only a small operation compared to the serious players so I was more on the edge of the action.

While I was in the air I got a text message to call home so when I landed I rang to check in with Samantha and wee Mack. But Samantha was super excited and could hardly wait to tell me the news that she'd bought a home for us. I was lost for words as this was supposed to be our dream home and we were planning to build it and without a single conversation together or viewing, she'd bought a house – well verbally anyway, the contract still had to be inked. To be fair it was a cracking deal as it was a new house that was about 80 per cent done, but the people who owned it had run into some difficulties and needed a quick sale, so she had jumped in. All that needed to be done was the landscaping and some interior things like window blinds.

When I got back from Vegas and saw it, I realised why Samantha had jumped in with both feet. It was a perfect pad and I signed on the dotted line. We would have probably built something similar if we'd started from scratch but we got ours for $485,000, when in reality it was worth a good chunk more than that. It was surrounded by this man-made lake and we had lovely glass sliding doors so you could walk out on to the balcony and look over the water. It had four bedrooms, four bathrooms, a study, solar panels on the roof – Glenrosa Children's Home it was not.

Now I look back, I think I was maybe being a bit of a prick as it was all a bit superficial and I think I wanted to show how well I'd done. To be fair, I was doing good and I had the money, so the two of us and our six-month-old pride and joy moved into our first proper family home – it would also be our last.

And just in case you're wondering, my lovely solid teak bed came with us and took pride of place in the master bedroom – and it's where I lay my head every night even now!

# 10

# Nightmare in Shanghai

ORGOTTEN was probably an apt name for the range, as I've since tried my level best to forget about it. While I stand by the quality of the actual bikes and their design, it wasn't the type of company I genuinely wanted to be part of. Things just didn't gel the way I wanted and I felt my partners were motivated by money. Granted, fresh air won't pay the bills and put food on the table – but to me, BMX is sacred and the riders deserve companies that put their heart and soul into their machines.

We were selling well, revenue was into the hundreds of thousands which wasn't bad going for a brand new name on the market, and we didn't have the spending power of the big guns to advertise, but we had my reputation and passion.

Maybe arrogantly, I think those were the real keys behind it.

But I wasn't seeing any extra cash filtering down. I was a part-owner and I felt I should have been seeing some of these big sales numbers coming into my own bank account. So I quizzed my partners and asked to see the books as I wanted to know what the hell was going on. If you own a company and it's flying, you want to know where the extra cash is going but they didn't let me see everything and it felt fishy to me. Something wasn't right and I wasn't given access to the paperwork to check it, but I let it go for a while and sort of convinced myself I was being paranoid.

That didn't stop me from taking a flamethrower to my personal life though when I was in Shanghai on business – that's where the bike factory was that made Forgotten.

It'd been eight months since Mackenzie was born but Samantha and I still hadn't started having sex again. Samantha never really got back into it after the sex ban during the pregnancy and I didn't complain but it did take a toll on me – I'm a red-blooded male.

I had a lot of emotional baggage wrapped up around sex. Maybe that's why I've chased so many girls in my time. But in China I sunk deep back into my deepest and darkest secret, something which I've never discussed and also kept hidden from Samantha. For a few reasons that trip brought it all back to me, and led to me taking a flamethrower to our marriage one last time.

My mind was back in the summer of 1977 and my good old Uncle Joe. He was one of those family friends who was so close he got called uncle, but we weren't actually related. I was out enjoying the hot weather and the long summer Scottish nights at the burn outside Joe's place and he shouted to me to come in for chocolate biscuits.

I knew him well – he used to spend a lot of time at our house and I had no issues or worries about putting my playtime on pause – so I sprinted in to enjoy some treats that were rarely on offer in the Craig household.

The treat I hadn't bargained for was that Joe wanted to have a little bit of playtime himself in what he called 'you touch me, I'll touch you'. I was only five years old and didn't think anything more about it than to get involved.

It began with Joe unzipping his trousers and asking me to take his penis out and give it a little rub. I trusted this man and felt safe around him, so I did it. There was me, this naive little boy standing there with this grown man's cock in my bare hands. It still sends shivers down my spine.

Then it was on to me as Joe got his grubby paws on my jeans, yanked down my zip and engulfed my wee penis in his big, sweaty hands. We stood there for what seemed like hours but it must have only been a few minutes, although it could well have been longer. Time seemed to be frozen as we masturbated each other – it's fucking disgusting to even admit it, never mind have the memory burned into my brain.

Suddenly I just felt out of my depth; something inside screamed this was not normal so I let go of his penis, pulled up my pants, quickly followed by my jeans. I ran out of the door and off back home ironically for safety, which is not a feeling I normally associated with our place.

I don't even remember the chocolate biscuits being that good which proves how much of it I've tried to block out, as a simple dry tea biscuit was normally all I got if I was lucky thanks to my clown of a father – so any form of chocolate was a seriously big deal.

Now as a man and a father, I look back on that day and admit that I was sexually abused. Uncle Joe had been grooming me, hanging around our house, getting friendly with me. It was all part of a cunning plan to win my trust and as a result, have my body as his own little plaything. I've no doubt he hoped that I'd react better and he'd be able to abuse me on a regular basis.

I can see I was the perfect target as I had a father who didn't care, my mother struggled by on a daily basis and I was desperately looking for attention. So I must have been a prime target.

I know logically that I did nothing wrong and I shouldn't blame myself but I can't help it. I've never seen him since that shameful day but for years this horrific dark secret gnawed away at me – and to be honest, it still is even today. I do feel it's one of the reasons why I went for jumps on ramps full throttle, spurred on by yet another painful childhood memory I wanted to somehow escape with the help of my magical BMX.

So all of that was swirling around in my mind in Shanghai and I brought it back to Australia with me. I was a ticking time bomb about to explode with all this sexual tension pulsating through me.

The straw that broke the camel's back came one day at home. I was still brooding about what I'd done and Samantha had this bee in her bonnet about taking pictures of Mackenzie. Sam seemed to think that she didn't like it but I liked to take pics of Mack daily as I wanted to look back on her as a beautiful baby before she grew up all too quickly. So I was snapping away and Samantha did her usual thing of nagging me, but I kept going, then she shouted, 'She doesn't like it.' I erupted and shouted back something like, 'You don't know what she likes, she's only nine months old and doesn't care about being photographed.' But I'd had it, I trooped towards our balcony, ripped open the glass doors and hurled my brand new Cannon G7 camera out towards the lake. I turned around and yelled, 'Are you fucking happy now?'

She came back and called me a psycho I think, then the red mist came down so I don't remember her words but she was giving me a right mouthful. And I don't know why I did this, but I grabbed her by the shoulders and began to shake her. I got into her face and snarled, 'Will you fucking listen?' Right then, the red mist went and I snapped back into reality and I was looking at my wife absolutely petrified. She was crying and I realised in that moment that I was out of control and thought, 'What the hell am I doing?' My daughter was sitting in her wee baby chair on this camel brown rug we had, looking up at her old man acting like a wild hyena.

I began saying I was sorry and tried to reassure Samantha. I didn't mean any danger to her, I was struggling with the guilt of what I'd done and worried I'd messed things up but she didn't want to know me right there and then. So she grabbed some things and Mackenzie – and drove over to her mum and dad's place, leaving me alone to contemplate what is one of the most shameful days of my life.

There I was in this lovely massive house which had made me feel like the king of the world only months earlier, and now I felt like all the air had been sucked out of my lungs. I was a walking zombie and I trudged down to the lake just to try to get some fresh air, and I stumbled across my camera. Even in my fit of rage I hadn't been able to throw it into the water.

I decided that I needed to get help so I ended up having some counselling, which did help me but it didn't really heal my wounds. Maybe that was down to me not being ready. I still loved Samantha and she did come back with Mackenzie – but remember, she didn't know about everything that was rattling about in my head. We tried to muddle on and things were okay but it wasn't the same. That bond had been broken and then it was shattered on Christmas Day 2008. It seems I have a thing for taking on massive, life-changing actions during the festive period.

As things weren't great, Samantha suggested we didn't get each other any presents for Christmas. The idea was to keep our cash and plough it into this fancy garden landscaping that we liked but maybe it was due to my guilt or just wanting to do something nice, I bought Samantha a watch – it cost me a few grand, it was Longines and had diamonds all around it. It looked pretty sharp but as I handed it over, her face looked like she'd just supped a glass of sour milk – then as she opened it, it was as if I'd handed her a turd in a box.

Her first words were, 'We could have landscaped the garden for this,' but I snapped back, 'This was my gift to you.' Fucking hell. I couldn't believe her attitude and it was like she wasn't willing to meet me halfway, so we had another argument, the usual back and forth. I had reached a high water mark and told Samantha, 'Look, if it's going to be like this all the time, I can't be in this marriage.' She said fine, called my bluff and that was it basically – our marriage was over. She again went off to her parents with Mackenzie and gave me seven days to clear out. To be fair, she did bring our daughter back during the day to see me and also to keep Mack in her routine.

I remember one day during that week, I went into the bathroom and just said to Samantha, 'Look, I don't want this.' I had thoughts of my biological dad being such a let-down to his family, I had thoughts of my adopted dad being such a great guy – all that was swirling around in my mind and I ended up in tears. Samantha told me to 'please leave' as she didn't want Mackenzie seeing her old man acting like a blubbering wreck – and I can see why.

But there really was no going back, I could see that. Like I've said, I take full responsibility for my mistake that set this chain of events in motion but I do feel Samantha didn't support me in some ways of being a father. Outside of my role as her husband, Samantha never gave me the comfort to be a dad. Maybe she didn't realise it but it was just as if she was Mackenzie's mother and I was not given the same status.

So with my marriage in tatters I had to think about the future and if I'm brutally honest, what was at the forefront of my mind? BMX will save me – that was what. Some people will wince reading this and imagine a man saying that. But I chose my sport over my wife and child and it kills me to admit that!

That was my focus as I knew there was another level I could get to in the sport, so I didn't want to lose any momentum and not reach that. Also I had my prized collection of Haro bikes from 1982 to 1993; Samantha didn't know how much I'd been collecting as I'd been buying them here, there and anywhere ever since I got to Australia. They were all in mint condition, either brand new or fully restored, so that was my priority and I thought that if I left them there I might never see them again. I couldn't bear that. I couldn't leave my BMX collection – but I could leave my wife and daughter.

It took me four trips to get it all out of the attic. I had my 4x4 packed full each time, but while you can take apart bikes there's only so far you can go. So I was driving 75 miles each way back into Melbourne to leave them with a friend for safe keeping. I admit that I should have been fighting for my marriage, but I wouldn't be where I am now if I had.

I still loved Samantha and Mackenzie but they couldn't understand what BMX meant to me. I'd put everything I had into my sport. I'd come from a horrendous background and it's what my focus had been all my life, since sitting in that cinema watching *ET*.

I can't say hand on heart that I regret how I acted at the end of our marriage. Lots of people will say that family is all that matters and blood is thicker than water but look at where I'd come from. I knew that was just a stupid fucking cliche and of course, Samantha never put me through anything close to the horror I'd suffered as a kid. But I couldn't live a lie.

I never admitted to her all of what I'd done and how I was sexually abused; I couldn't change the past and I know now after going through more counselling, I had to accept that – but I couldn't and she couldn't offer me a way to stay. Whether that was emotionally or in other ways, I wasn't going to reach my peak in BMX if I'd stayed. So rightly or wrongly, I left feeling I had to and you know what, professionally it was the best move I ever made. I think with the distraction of my personal guilt on the back burner, I saw things more clearly at

Forgotten and the feelings I felt before surrounding the issues of my ten per cent commission returned, only this time stronger.

I decided that enough was enough as I felt I had given them the benefit of the doubt twice. I'd tried to make it work but I didn't feel we were really partners and it was all my nous that was making Forgotten work. I confronted them and said, 'Buy me out,' but they claimed not to have the cash. So I said, 'Right, I'll get a loan and buy you out.' But they didn't want to sell and it dragged on back and forth – and I was getting ground down and down. I was scunnered by it. We'd had good times with Triplesix and then into Forgotten, but I couldn't keep swallowing my pride and working as hard as I could for a cause I didn't have any trust in and eventually I told them, 'I need out – and I need out now.'

So they offered to pay me for 25 per cent of the company. What I finally got was a joke and it was worth a lot more and I knew it – but I'd come to the end of the road. I wanted them out of my life and to be free of a company I didn't feel represented me – and now I was free in my professional life, as well as my personal one too.

\* \* \* \* \*

I kicked off 2009 by going on a boys' trip to Brisbane. I guess I thought it would help me get a fresh start and time to cool down. One of my mates, Paul Everest, had a condom company but he'd got 500 delivered with a typo on their packaging so it read 'remium condoms'. He gave them to me for the trip – God knows what he thought I'd be doing. But I never used one. I could barely talk to a girl for the two weeks I was away, which was not normal for me. Eager to get back to my young, free and single image, I shaved my hair into a mohawk. I must have looked like a real idiot, trying to pretend I was loving life. But I wasn't – I was miserable.

Once I got back though, I decided the only thing to do was launch my own BMX range but this time, with just me in control and making all the big decisions. I called it Pilgrim, which was a nod to my days back in Dundee. It was a concept I'd always liked and I felt it was fitting to base it on my days when I really started to ride properly and began dedicating my life to the sport.

So I had the name and the ethos but starting a company isn't as simple as all that. I needed cash to get a website set up, create advertising and put in place an infrastructure. After all my experience I knew what was required, but getting the funds was another matter. I had to ask my family and once again they stepped up for me.

My parents, along with some aunts and uncles, lent just over $100,000 to get Pilgrim off the ground. I was less worried about the actual bikes, as I lived and breathed that, so I ploughed all the cash into all the other things. I got a great Pilgrim logo which kind of looks like two nuns kissing – I still sometimes marvel at it today, it's really snazzy and I wanted the bikes to be the same.

It's not as hard to design a bike as you'd think, if you know how.

The top tube which connects the seat to the handlebars is either 20.5, 20.75 or 21 inches, the chainstay which runs from the crank to the back wheel is 13.75 inches normally and then your bottom bracket is 13.5 inches off the ground – so you've got clearance when you're pedalling around a corner so your feet don't drag along the road. With those sort of basics in place, then you decide what kind of look you want; you can add details in, you can work on colour schemes.

I got a lot of help from my old friend Clint Millar. He owns Colony BMX so he filled me in and helped me avoid some of the pitfalls that a new range might typically suffer. I didn't want to use my family's money on buying loads of stock so I hatched another plan. I designed five models – Protégé, Civilian, Drifter, Pioneer and Quest – I settled on them after getting the opinions of people in the industry on over 50 names. I did each in two colour schemes and ordered them to be built in Taiwan as that's where the high end bikes are all made, even today. It only cost me a few grand to get my samples but once they arrived, I used the infrastructure I'd paid for to get together some slick-looking brochures and all that.

Then I went back to all my old customers and showed them what I had as they all knew me, but more importantly they trusted me because I'd always stuck to my vow of never endorsing anything I wouldn't ride, and they jumped on board. So my first proper order to Taiwan was way over six figures, which was a pretty big commitment for a brand with no history – and you pay before the bikes are shipped, so I did a deal with my customers. I said if my customers paid up front, I'd knock 20 per cent off the price.

The shops were in as it was a good deal and I had built in a 50 per cent mark-up so I was still in the black – and the factory got paid in advance of shipping. So as a result when the freight landed in Melbourne, I'd already sold the lot. I had set up international bank accounts and had an accountant so Pilgrim was up and running with a bang.

I guess it was a lot for someone with no education to take on but I knew BMX so well, and the other business side was really just common sense. I had to find out how to organise international payments when ordering stock from Taiwan. Once I did, I really took it all in, I understood what was happening and I did the same with anything else that came up. It really was a moment of satisfaction to think that me grinding on some steps in Dundee had been turned into a proper BMX company that was churning out quality bikes – and even better, the people who were buying them were giving me rave reviews.

Things had also improved with Samantha. I'd moved out but I was still paying the mortgage and making sure she and Mackenzie were looked after. Stevie McCann had given me his house to live in, as he was over in the

States. Now he was in the big time, Stevie didn't have to bother but he told me to go round and get his keys from his parents. So I was in this five-bedroom pad, down the coast in a small town called Blairgownie. Each room had four beds; Stevie liked a party and had kitted the place out specifically for that but it was just me rattling around in there; I didn't throw parties as I was busy making sure Pilgrim capitalised on its early promise. Being able to live there rent-free really helped me out and it was touching to have a pal come through like that.

I still wanted Samantha back and maybe the space had given us both time to think. We were in regular contact and things progressed to the point of Samantha suggesting we meet every weekend but then it ended up being only once every two weeks. From where I was in Blairgownie, it was a four-hour drive or a 50-minute ferry to Ocean Grove, where our family house was, and we'd have nice days where we would go for lunch or just hang out.

Samantha was impressed that I'd kept up paying the bills and had not let them down. I had betrayed her but I took my role as providing for and protecting both of them seriously and I was even sometimes allowed to sleep over in the house. Not in the same bedroom of course, but in the master bedroom as she hadn't been using it anyway – she'd sleep downstairs to be closer to Mackenzie. It was nice but it didn't seem to be going anywhere romantically as all kissing or touching was firmly out of bounds.

But because I was living in this nice big pad on my own, outside of Pilgrim I had nothing to occupy my time – I was a single guy essentially with nothing outside of work to do, except every second weekend. So I ended up surfing the net, talking to girls and what not. I was meeting up with some of them, I won't lie about that, but I still hoped Samantha and I had a chance. I'd even managed to finally landscape our property and that cost me a few bob. All in all I spent around $50,000 on it, but it looked unreal!

It had a ten-seat spa bath with swim jets and we got the Merbau decking, which is the Rolex of that world. It looked like it was out of a home magazine and I was glad little Mackenzie would have fun larking about there and Samantha again was impressed I'd stepped up. I was on the way back on both fronts – but the Buultjens train was set to come off the rails in spectacular style.

# 11

# Goodbye Mackenzie

W ITH Pilgrim going from strength to strength, I was buzzing and I'd also recruited a lot of the top riders in the southern hemisphere. To illustrate that, at the 2011 X Games there were nine medals up for grabs and Pilgrim riders walked away with four. Stevie McCann was one of them; he was my landlord but I was his boss – what a complicated relationship!

The team was also made up of Jed Mildon, Cam Pianta, Vince Byron, Dane Searls, Matt Whyatt, Jaie Toohey, Andrew Ahumada and Logan Martin, who are all without doubt among the best BMX riders on the face of the earth today.

All these guys are still pro and go around the world with Nitro Circus – and they started out with me.

Andrew was one of the youngest riders I got to know; he was about 11 when we met.

The thing was I didn't really scout riders or go out of my way to find a certain type of character. I'd be at the skateparks, either doing demos, filming or just having a laugh and I'd see these kids.

I could see which ones had the X-factor to go further as a lot of being a pro is about what you do off the bike. You can be the best rider or the most skilled, and of course that will take you places but to really cut through, you need the personality to go with it.

Andrew had that and he was so good at a young age that he was nicknamed 'Mini Mirra'. It actually pissed me off when Samantha mentioned that some of the neighbours around Ocean Grove had commented about me hanging about with kids. She said I was a grown man and it was odd.

We all know what they were insinuating but I didn't have time for that narrow-minded nonsense as I was basically trying to help the boys out. If I had a contact that might do them some good or maybe an opportunity I knew about, or if I could give them a lift to a contest as they were too young to drive – I did it. It wasn't me secretly trying to gain their trust or me hoodwinking them into riding for Pilgrim. I was just being me, I was the same as them – only older. And when I got Pilgrim, they were keen to join, and I was keen to have them.

I met Jed in a skate park while I was over in New Zealand on the North Island. He's a proud Maori and from this little place called Taupo – and he's passionate about representing his culture when he's riding. We kept in touch and that's how he became a Pilgrim rider, and he also made history on one of my bikes. Jed pulled off the first ever triple backflip on a BMX in 2011. It was sensational.

Jed had told me he trusted me so much that he wanted to do it on my bike. The actual jump has been viewed nearly ten million times on YouTube alone, and Jed has since gone on to break more records – which I was involved in.

Another superstar I had on Pilgrim was Dane Searls, whose speciality was mega-high jumps. It took 18 months to prepare for his own world record when he pulled off the biggest ever dirt jump on a BMX. Dane was so far up in the air at one point that he was actually above the helicopter filming him.

These stunts were serious affairs and Dane's record cost about $250,000 all in as one big cost was clean dirt to build the hills that he was launching from, as it needed to be free of any glass, rocks or stones, then there was all the filming and other things around it. It was Paul who shelled out for Dane and Jed's records. At least he got a return on them and helped push his Unit Clothing brand, which was a far better idea than the 500 'remium condoms' he gave me after my marriage ended. I'm still in contact with all my riders today, as well as Paul, because we were really all mates first, and colleagues second.

Sadly, however, Dane tragically passed away shortly after conquering his largest jump ever. He'd been out celebrating at a nightclub on the Gold Coast, which was one level up, and down below was a swimming pool, so livewire Dane wanted to jump right into the pool but unfortunately a bouncer saw him just as he was about to do it and grabbed his t-shirt. The result was that Dane's momentum was halted and he ended up crashing head first into the concrete area around the pool. He battled bravely in a coma for a week before passing away. It still sends a shiver down my spine when I think about it as he'd always said that he wanted to go out on his bike – and to die after falling from 20 feet in a silly accident, when he was used to doing 60-foot stunts without blinking an eye, was truly tragic.

I thought of Dane when I had a horrific fall and broke my neck when I was riding at The Shed in Melbourne. I went full-on into a trick, but it didn't quite come off. I went down hard and in hospital they saw I'd fractured my C1, C2 and C3 vertebrae – plus my teeth were smashed to pieces. It was a real sore one and could have ended my life and being in a wheelchair was also more than a possibility.

I know why it happened and it had nothing to do with my skill or ability to do the jump. Once I'd recovered, I went back 12 months later and nailed it, just to prove to myself what I already knew. The first time I had been too relaxed, I was in my comfort zone and I wasn't on the edge.

And to be a BMXer, you need that tension; you can't be riding up the ramp and feeling everything is great. Well, I certainly can't. I need it to be a serious situation that I'm all-in, fully committed to and since I was scraped up off the concrete that day I've adopted that idea. I won't ever slip into the comfort zone like that. I don't mean that I want every day to be a total helter-skelter but I do want to feel like I'm striving, like I'm jumping off a 40-foot ramp and trying to pull off a trick I haven't quite mastered.

In the end I had 18 athletes signed to Pilgrim and I saw myself in each and every one of them. The same way I wouldn't endorse a bike that I wouldn't ride, I wouldn't sign a rider I didn't admire.

A lot of what makes them great is what they do off the bike. Some guys are super-talented but get carried away and become arrogant and that's going to bite you in the backside in BMX.

For example, our X Games medal success resulted in no increase in sales at Pilgrim. You'd think logically it would but no, whereas on the other hand if someone like Jed or Mini Mirra took the time to write back to some kid on Facebook or Twitter, that would.

That kid can't be doing triple backflips in their garden and they can't be pulling off super-skilled tricks without years of honing their craft. The top pros like Jed, Andrew, Matt and Jaie are at a level that's unattainable for most kids – they'll never get there but they can touch all of them with their personalities.

BMX has really been affected by the digital revolution and the old way of moving bikes or building brands soon became defunct so what worked in 2000 didn't work in 2011 – and certainly doesn't in 2017. But I didn't have to worry, I had a great squad of lads. They were dynamite on the bike and electric off it – we had the whole game sewn up.

I kept reordering from Taiwan ever year for my new models and mostly they were sold before they were even loaded into their shipping containers. I was really riding the crest of a wave with Pilgrim but then my agent there Leo informed me he'd made a major cock-up by accident; he'd submitted my order twice meaning that instead of 800 bikes, I was getting 1,600. I had the cash to cover my original order but I didn't have the same again to just hand over to him.

Everything had run smoothly previously so I wanted to help him out as in some ways, we were in it together and I took on the extra 800 but didn't pay up front for them. I agreed to pay him as they sold but the thing was, I couldn't just double demand overnight. BMX was in a real purple patch so there was plenty of competition and I didn't have the marketing budgets of the big boys.

I hustled as best I could and I did sell some of the extras, but with storage costs and freight bills, it was costing me big time to simply keep them. I let the last 600 go for a song, I think less than 50 per cent of what I was paying Leo for them, and as they say in business, cash is king – which is all too true.

The squeeze really hurt me and I was in a jam. I was pretty bitter as I'd got myself into a hole to help out Leo. I felt I'd sucked a vat of lemons when I found out that he'd done this 'double order shuffle' with other brands like We The People and Eastern. So it wasn't an honest mistake, but pure greed on his part and it was too late to kick up a stink. I'd taken the extra bikes and sent his money over. I kept battling on though and ended up back out at Interbike in Vegas, which wasn't a very eventful trip as I was just trying to make contacts and build Pilgrim.

But I touched back down in Melbourne, turned on my phone and noticed a picture to my horror on my Facebook. While Samantha and I were meeting up I'd started seeing a petite girl called Sharon, better known as Shazza, and she'd been out for Halloween while I was away and had dressed up as Catwoman. I suspect she'd had a few drinks and she took a pic of her in the skin-tight suit and wrote on my wall, 'This little pussy can't wait until she comes home and gets served by you.'

With the time difference and travelling, it had been up there for about 15 hours by the time I saw it and someone showed it to Samantha, or she saw it herself – and she went apeshit. I got a real blast and she told me that she couldn't believe I was fucking around when we were trying to piece things together. With Shazza it was never going to be a serious relationship, we were more spending time together and having a laugh. I know it's easy to say that but I was lonely too, being on my own.

Either way, Samantha was not willing to take any more and we struggled on for a few more months and into the New Year. Then when Samantha delivered the bombshell that it was over forever on 18 January 2011, which ironically was Mackenzie's fourth birthday. There was no going back and it was also the last time I saw my daughter. I end up almost in tears every time I think about the fact, that I haven't been a part of her life since then. I've tried to see her but Samantha would say that Mackenzie didn't want to.

It came up during our divorce as I'd been served the papers with Samantha's lawyer asking for 75 per cent of the house and our savings, plus 50 per cent of my pension. I was a broken man and the finality of it all was tough to deal with. I felt like a punch-drunk boxer, reeling from the body blows. I told them I would sign it, they could have taken everything for all I cared.

In the court, I asked the judge about Mackenzie but she told me that the hearing was only about finances, children were not part of it. I did look into getting a family lawyer but it was going to cost around $125,000 for me and the same for Samantha. I genuinely didn't want to land us both with that sort of debt and I didn't want to fight with Samantha or cause Mackenzie any more unhappiness. It would only put her under stress and I wanted to be her father that she enjoyed being around, not some guy who'd dragged her through all sorts of stress and legal hearings. I kept calling Samantha and leaving messages, I pleaded with her to get round the table and at least work out some way I could visit my daughter – as she had to come first before our break-up.

But Samantha refused, and still does, and would not budge an inch. I think the guilt of knowing what I'd done made me become a bit more defeatist and eventually I got the message so I thought I'd just work my bollocks off to prove to Samantha that Mackenzie was better off with me in her life, rather than out of it.

I want to communicate and I'm sure my wee girl misses me. As I write this, she'll now be ten, so it's been six years since I've seen her. It's the same for my parents, who have both lost out on being grandparents in lots of ways. They have met Mack and I treasure the one photo I've got of them doing that. In my parents' living room in Monifieth – they've since moved again, it's a small town on Scotland's east coast – all the pictures I've sent them over the years of Mackenzie are either on the walls or sitting proudly in frames.

They still send gifts every year on her birthday and at Christmas to Samantha's parents' address, but even so they never get a reply nor any acknowledgement whatsoever – and that's another thing about this situation that breaks my heart.

But I feel this book and the movie about my life will help the healing process for us all as I want to show Mackenzie that I've always tried to do my best and follow my heart. I have this odd feeling of Mack picking up this book one day or watching my movie and finding out what her dad is really like – not whatever she's been told about me, as she was too young to have formed her own opinion in many ways.

There's no feeling in the world like pulling off a massive jump or trick on a BMX. It really is on another level. As a father I say the same about a hug from your own child. Nothing compares to it – I just wish I'd experienced it a lot more often.

# 12

# But You're Not American

T HE order scandal at Pilgrim had really jammed me up and I did my best to soldier on but it really was getting hard to meet all the commitments as I'd essentially paid out double what I'd planned to without bringing in anything close to that. Money was tight and I was still paying the mortgage on the family home as our divorce had been sorted out.

I had left Stevie's place and was living with Jarred Dowson. Ironically it was Shazza – who'd put the final nail in my marriage's coffin – who kept Pilgrim operational as while her social media intrusion hadn't done me any favours, her friend Thea Groom owned this company called Leaf Busters.

Thea was in her late 50s and looked just like Heather Locklear – and did her own zany TV adverts, as she'd come up with this fire-resistant mesh that you fitted over the gutters. Bush fires are a real issue in Australia and New Zealand and quite often, it's the embers from those fires that land in gutters and ignite dried leaves. Once the roof catches fire it's nigh-on impossible to save the house.

So it was a great product and I did a bit of research on it as just like my bikes, I wasn't going to work with anything I didn't believe in. I did the training programme, learned how to measure and fit it and then began work for Leaf Busters where I was back to being on commission.

I kept it very quiet as I didn't want my athletes worrying or my competitors trying to grab my market share if they saw I was on my knees financially. Leaf Busters really kept the show on the road. I was making good money and started going around the city and showing it to householders, then I'd take that cash and pump it into Pilgrim.

I remember one time in New Zealand, I'd done a few Leaf Busters jobs there and I was taking cash out of my wallet and handing it over to Jed, as he was still my rider – he was one of the few people I trusted and I'd told him what was going on. Jed didn't want to take it but I insisted. I carried on doing that, but things just weren't sustainable. I subconsciously realised that Pilgrim would have to end, as I was driving quickly down a cul-de-sac.

And things came to an almighty head on 1 January 2012 when – and it's hard to admit this – I wanted to end it all.

I had a hard time admitting it for a while, but that's precisely what I tried to do. Things had just gotten to the point where I couldn't see any way out; it's a bit like the analogy of seeing a light at the end of the tunnel, only to realise it's an oncoming train. With my business and personal life ending up in the crapper, that's how I felt. I wasn't lonely for people to be around, I was lonely in terms of intimacy and I couldn't see how I'd reach my goals anymore.

I spent New Year's Day with my good mate Dean Druce and there was a party going on at Robbie Maddison's family's place in Nowra up in New South Wales as he was about to do one of his famous New Year stunts for Red Bull live on TV. Robbie is a global star as he's the guy who jumped Tower Bridge in London with a backflip – he was Daniel Craig's stunt double for the motorbike scenes in the James Bond thriller *Skyfall* too. And he did this amazing stunt not long ago where he rode a motorbike on a giant wave, like he was surfing on it.

Anyway, that New Year's Day Robbie was planning on jumping 400 feet across San Diego Bay but in the end he only did 378 feet and nine inches – because of the damp conditions. So it was a nice vibe, us all cheering him on, but as I left to drive back to Melbourne, I was on the Hume Highway. It hit me hard and I just thought, 'How the fuck did my life end up turning to shit?'

I put my foot hard on the gas, closed my eyes and just waited for what was coming next, whether that was smashing into a heavy goods truck or careering off the road. I didn't know – but I wanted it to end there and then.

'Wake up, daddy.' That's what shocked my brain back to life. I heard my wee Mackenzie pleading with me and my eyes sprang open. I was doing 120km an hour but I gripped the wheel and slowed down as the tears were streaming down my face. So Mackenzie, thank you – you saved your old man, even though you didn't know it.

Then, not long afterwards, the most amazing thing happened that hit me like a bolt from the blue and I was back on top of my game. It was a zero to hero moment as my world just spun on its axis and my blood was pumping again. I'll never forget it.

One day I was sprawled out in Jarred's living room – I'd turned it into a cinema den with my big TV and speakers – when my phone burst into action. It was my old colleague Steve Paraskevas. Initially when I saw the caller ID, I sort of panicked as I thought maybe he'd heard about Pilgrim's struggles and was on to offer some words of consolation – which would have made me feel even worse. But he just said, 'John, your dream job has come up.'

I didn't have a clue what he was talking about. He went on to explain that Haro was looking for a new global brand manager – and he was putting me up for it. Steve had carried on in the industry behind the scenes and was now Haro's main man in Australia, so he had a direct line to their head office over in Vista, southern California.

I was searching for words and sort of managed to force out my agreement. Bloody hell, this was the brand that had founded Freestyle BMX, that had got me into the sport and it had always been my dream to work there. But to be in the running for the top job there, being the face of the brand – that was another level.

Once I'd hung up I took a few minutes just to take it all in. This was mega and it really would see me at the top of the tree, becoming a serious big-name player in the BMX world. I'd always felt like the underdog, battling and scrapping for everything I got, but this would really put me on a whole new level. You only got one chance at this sort of thing so I was definitely committed.

A few days later, after Steve had done his thing, Haro's president Joe Hawk rang me. He recalled we'd met briefly the previous year in Taiwan when I'd been out there on Pilgrim business and he'd been there with Haro. He mentioned how he'd been really impressed with what I'd done with my own brand and admired what it was built on – but then he took the wind out of my sails. He informed me that Haro's shareholders wanted an American; that was the clear message, it had to be someone from the States.

What a kick in the plums. Here was this opportunity of a lifetime, the best role in BMX without a doubt, I'd been recommended and my bloody nationality had ruled me out.

But I wasn't going to accept that, not after what I'd sacrificed. I'm the guy who had chosen BMX over his wife and daughter so I knew there was more out there in the sport for me – and this was it.

I wasn't going to just let it slip through my fingers so I told Joe, 'I understand what you're saying but please give me an interview.' That's all I asked for but he didn't want to waste my time or mess me about so I said it again, 'give me an interview' – I wanted to show him what I could do.

So he agreed, but again reminded me of this American-only rule, and I just blanked that bit out. I had my way in and as soon as we hung up, I went online and immediately booked my flight. It cost me $2,100 to fly from Melbourne to Los Angeles and then another $700 for a hire car to get down to Haro's HQ – and a few days later I was off.

Logically it was madness. I'd just spent $2,800 of my own money, when really I needed to be belt tightening, to go to an interview on the other side of the world for a job that I'd been told clearly by the company's president I had no chance of getting.

Fuck it – I'd always relished a challenge.

* * * * *

I knew I had to be proactive to get around this American-only rule and one ace up my sleeve was my Haro collection, which I'd been building up for years. It had been in storage since I left Samantha – no one else on the planet had anything like it. I thought that the people at Haro needed to know I was passionate and serious about the challenge – plus I wanted the whole world to know.

So I built all the bikes up; I fitted all the tyres and I asked my pal Pete Robbins, who owned The Shed Skatepark in Melbourne, if he could shut it off to the public for 15 minutes for me. Once he knew what I was doing he agreed and I basically showcased my collection from 1982, the first year Haro made a BMX, through to 1993. There's no other collection like it anywhere else. Some people have lots of bikes but they might need to take the wheels off one to fit on to the other, or share the parts – mine are all complete.

It took seven days to build them all and transport them to The Shed, and for just 15 minutes. They were all in mint condition and I've never ridden any of them. I move them by picking up and carrying them, and even then I wipe down the tyres when I pack them away again. Thankfully I had some good friends there with me; Lindsay Brown, Damien Bowerman and Ryan Bishop, so the boys helped me put the bikes in place as well as filming and taking photos of my collection.

The video went down a storm and created some hype, which I know got back to the team at Haro, and the key thing was that it wasn't coming from me directly but the BMX world. They were all buzzing about it.

It really helped prove I was the right man to lead the brand and the only thing I did feel bad about was when

I finally moved to Haro, that video kept getting more views for a while than some of the clips online of the pro riders there. And it really was just some beaten-up, old BMX guy chatting about a bunch of old bikes. It's still up online today.

Call me deranged, but I just had the feeling that the job was for me as Haro was what had got me into BMX. I'd worked in the bakery and did a paper round just to buy my first Haro but I couldn't think of anything better than being the main man at Haro. Joe Hawk realised I'd shelled out a small fortune just to come over so he paid for my hotel.

After jetting into LAX, I got to the hotel as fast as I could and had a quick shower. It was a Wednesday and I went out for Mexican food with Joe, Pete Garski, Haro's international sales manager, and James Ayres, the domestic sales manager. It was all nice and friendly but we didn't really talk shop or get into things too much; it was more just to break the ice. After that I headed back to the hotel to get my head down. I was shattered as it'd been a whirlwind few weeks from getting the news to actually being in the US and within touching distance of my dream.

The next day I went into Haro HQ. For me that was like a pilgrimage; stepping on to that hallowed turf was akin to a nun going to Lourdes. It was a seriously big deal and Joe was smart with the way he played it, taking a bit of a back seat and letting the staff interview me. So the people I'd be in charge of were the ones giving me the

Spanish inquisition, and I realised Joe would then be getting their feedback to help him in making a decision. It was a good move as I needed to be part of a team and we all had to work together. Plus, if they didn't respect me, there's no way they'd follow my lead and get behind the way I wanted to direct the brand.

I thought I'd get a break and maybe come back the next day for a one on one with Joe. But no, he took me to a lunch with a close associate of the majority shareholders, who are from Taiwan. He was a guy from Harvard and pretty polished and later on, Joe told me that he thought I was a bit raw but Joe replied that I was a BMX kid, I was rough and ready. That's what the action sports world is all about, we're not the classy, elegant sort of folk.

Then we got back in the car and Joe headed to the head office of the shoe company Vans, bringing me along for the ride. I went in with him as they were working on a Haro-inspired sneaker and I was listening to their conversation, but I wasn't feeling the design. Never one to hold my tongue, I jumped in and told them what I thought, I said how I'd do it and then talked about doing a bike to match the shoe.

Looking back, what the hell was I thinking? I was there as a spectator and had no place to be chipping in but I think Joe respected that and really saw how much Haro meant to me. I wanted them to produce the best sneaker as Haro is such a special brand – nothing in BMX comes close. I felt that way even though I wasn't making a penny off the sneaker and they could easily use my input and pack me off back to Melbourne, never to see me again.

Anyway it seemed to sit well, Joe had no plans that night so he suggested we went for a meal – and we ended up in this nice Italian place. I spoke about what I wanted to bring to the job and where I felt Haro was lacking and needed improvement but then for some reason and maybe it's because we were having spaghetti, but *The Lady and The Tramp* sprang into my mind. I couldn't resist so I grabbed Joe's hand and said, 'Isn't this romantic?'

He must have thought I was a lunatic as this was me on an interview for the number one BMX job, but it still was a corporate role. I didn't suggest we eat the same piece of spaghetti from opposite ends – even for me, that was a step too far. If I'd known him better though, maybe I would. Thankfully Joe agreed with me and joked it was the perfect evening.

On the Friday I was back into Haro again, facing Joe and talking about my obsession with the brand, but the main thing I wanted to get over was how I felt Haro needed to be Haro. I felt it was being everything else but Haro. It was the leader and the BMX brand that everyone loved but it had lost its magic, the bikes weren't special. I felt it had to be brought back to what it was and I knew I could do that.

As I left to head back to LAX, the interview that was supposed to be a one-hour chat had ended up as a two-and-a-half-day performance. I asked Joe, 'Am I what you're looking for?' and he replied, 'You're a whole lot more.' Even thinking about that now chokes me up; it meant so much to me. The president of Haro could understand what the brand meant to me and was going to convince the shareholders to relent on this non-American issue.

Just before I flew out, I went up to see my mate Xavier Mendez, an old-school rider and serious player in BMX. He is great friends with all the big riders from the 1980s like Mat Hoffman, Mike Dominguez and Brian Blyther. We got to know each other over the years so I spent the Friday night at his place. I told him about the job at Haro and he was blown away for me. I said the signs were good but I'd have to work on a visa as being Scottish, I was going to have to apply to be allowed to work in the US.

His wife Cari overhead us and blurted out that she had a contact, attorney Kelly O'Reilly, who specialised in that. We both shouted at the same time that Cari should give her a call – and she did, just after correcting us that it was a male Kelly. He was receptive and said that if I got the green light from Haro, I could get him to handle my application.

So as I flew back, I felt really satisfied; I'd given it everything and it paid off. I was only back in Melbourne for a few weeks when Joe told me that I had got the job but the only issue was the visa. So I didn't let myself go crazy and celebrate but my dream job was so close I could taste it, although far enough away that it could sail right by me.

I was straight on to Kelly and told him to get the wheels in motion and he explained to me that it was a simple equation of having to prove to the US government that no American could do the job like me. The other negative was that I had no degrees. My only qualification was in hotel management – and cooking a good Scottish breakfast isn't really relevant when it comes to running a BMX brand. I scrambled about trying to find people I thought would be in a good position to speak on my behalf.

Looking back at the letters, I can't believe who stepped up for me. One big one was from a representative of the BMX Olympic Committee, Shannon Gillette, who wrote a really strong piece about how much I knew and how much Haro meant to me. And then out of the blue, fucking Bob Haro himself wrote about me. This was the guy who got me into BMX when I saw him riding his bike back in 1982 in that Glasgow cinema as I stared open-mouthed at *ET*. Bob wrote that I knew more about Haro than even he did. I also got a letter from Clint Millar who stated that he'd love to get me for his company, but couldn't afford me.

It was all powerful stuff and I ended up with 12 in the end. I read them again for this book and I ended up in tears as to see my heroes and BMX legends talk about this wee kid from Glasgow in that way was simply beyond comprehension.

All of that was fired over to Kelly and he set about pleading my case. He told me that it'd be about a six-month wait and I'd decided that I didn't want to stay in Melbourne – or Australia, for that matter – much longer.

\* \* \* \* \*

The cash situation at Pilgrim had killed the company and I wasn't able to recover it but I couldn't just shut up shop and walk away. In Australia if you go bankrupt, you have to hand in your passport so that was not an option for me with my eyes being firmly fixed on heading to the US.

I wasn't going to do that anyway as that would have been a coward's way out – plus I owed a lot of cash to my own family, and as it happened my mum was over visiting her family in Perth. I flew over there and laid it all out on the table for them as I wanted to tell them the exact state of play. There were two options; either I kept going with Leaf Busters until I paid them back all the money I owed them, or close Pilgrim and I'd promise to get their money back to them as soon as I could – as I'd go to Haro and work my bollocks off until they had it all back. Again, my family left me dumbfounded with their understanding and compassion. They told me, 'Don't worry about paying us back, sort yourself out and give it to us when you can.'

I went back to Melbourne almost in shock as these people were once again backing me to the hilt. I think maybe if I'd hadn't just gone through my divorce and also been banned from seeing Mackenzie, I might have been able to see a way out for Pilgrim to survive – but I wasn't in that sort of place. So it ended after an amazing three-year run and I totalled up that my overall loss was $165,000 to close the business. I had to cover this – and I did.

The only person I didn't make whole was that sneaky fucker Leo. I owed him $10,000 and I wasn't going to fork out for that as he'd sold me down the river and I'd paid most of his cash before I discovered this accidental ordering was an old trick of his.

I'm glad that I never lowered standards at Pilgrim to keep the lights on, like selling lower-quality bikes or skimping on the designs. I look back with real pride on it and at the time I was aware that I had ruffled some feathers of the big boys. The distributors and agents had filtered word back to the boardrooms that this small company was really punching above its weight. What they didn't know, is that I was on my arse – I wasn't broke but a lot of the money I'd built up had gone.

And because I'd used my own initiative like with my Haro collection video, Joe was also keen to keep me in the loop so he invited me to come to The BMX World's in Cologne that July, as an international guest of Haro. This was a no-brainer as it was Haro's 30th anniversary and everyone who was anyone in BMX was going to be there to celebrate it. Yes, it was going to cost me a bit of cash – but I was getting paid to turn up and it kept my push forward for the job going strong. Plus I wasn't going to miss the chance to be at such a historic event that I would have happily gone to sit in the crowd and watch.

I'd barely arrived in Germany and was checking in at the hotel when my heroes like Mat, Mike, Brian, Ron Wilkerson, along with Xavier, came rolling by. They saw me and came right over of course and said, 'Do you want to go to Amsterdam?' I could barely keep my eyes open, but who's going to turn down a European road trip with their idols? So I dumped my bags and jumped in the car and we had a crazy night smoking weed and drinking loads of stuff, so I don't have too clear a memory of what we did because of that.

I do remember the way back though – the whole point of the exercise had been to pick up the old Haro MC Kevin Martin, who was on holiday there, and I was in agony as I ended up in the back of the car and as I've mentioned, my knees are shot so I can't sit cramped up like that. But I really felt I couldn't say anything as all these legends of the sport have been banged up way worse than me, and I was still sort of in shock at being part of their gang. So I grinned and beared it, thankfully I got the middle, so I could kind of stretch out over the handbrake – and it was a fantastic thing to be a part of.

Seeing all the old riders doing their thing, as the organisers had built the old-school 1980s-style ramps, was surreal and even the current stars of the sport stopped and watched them in awe. There was so much respect for the older crew and what they'd created with their legacy – everyone else in the sport has just been standing on their shoulders.

On the final night we all went out for dinner and I ended up next to Bob Haro. It was the first time we'd really had a chat, although I met him once before in 2009 when I'd bought him dinner, which was the least I could do and the only thing I could offer to show my gratitude for what he'd helped build. I had chicken schnitzel, but I can't recall what Bob ate. I didn't bring up that I was angling to take over being the BMX face of his brand but it was nice to just be around the guy.

From there we all went back to Haro HQ in Vista after an intense day of flights, which short-circuited my body clock as I had breakfast in Zurich, lunch in Vancouver and dinner in Los Angeles. They wanted me to come out and see the launch of the 2013 range in the Hyatt Hotel, close to the office, and they were doing the presentation to all the sales reps in the ballroom. Joe led it as he does every year and went through the details of what the new models were all about. Then he introduced me, saying I was the most passionate guy and biggest Haro fan on the planet, and I felt a bit shy getting all these compliments in front of a room of complete strangers but I got up and said I was due to be the new global brand manager when my visa application was approved – that probably should have been if, but I was the eternal optimist.

After the formal bit, we all sort of mingled and it was a key chance for me to get some valuable insight from the reps but it was all whinge, whinge, whinge. They didn't really like the bikes and said they weren't that popular with customers, they were lacking something, and I totally understood their drift. I agreed but I didn't want to get too mouthy with criticism until my feet were firmly under the desk, although it did chime with my thinking. I wanted to get people's excitement levels back and make Haro what it should be and bring back that lustre and shine, so when you sit on a Haro, you feel special and just want to ride the hell out of it.

I also did some stuff with the American media and online BMX websites. They interviewed me as a pro rider and international guest – and on my final night, Joe, Bob Haro and I all went out for a beer. Bear in mind that I was still sort of on a job interview – but I hadn't followed any of those rules until that point, so why start then?

We were at this bar called The Cracken and I led the charge as we went in and ordered the drinks. While I did that I told the barmaid, 'You're fucking gorgeous.' She was good looking but I've no idea why I said it, I just blurted it out, although she seemed to like it and leaned over the bar then kissed me passionately – it was some serious tonsil hockey. Next thing, she dragged me into the back storeroom and we were all over each other like a rash for about ten minutes, but Joe and Bob were still standing there with parched sandpaper throats. Eventually I staggered back to them with my clothes still intact somehow and we had a nice evening, just chewing the fat.

As we were leaving, this exotic-looking Peruvian princess by the name of Martita Gastiaburu caught my eye. She was with a big group of females but brushed me off and told me, 'I'm taken, talk to one of my friends.' But I wanted to talk to her and eventually she let slip that she was a hairdresser and that she enjoyed doing triathlons so there was a bike connection and boom – I can talk about bikes to any person on the planet for as long as they can keep their eyes open.

We hit it off, but I had to tell her that I'd love to take her out in about six months and she thought I was off my head. I explained that I was coming back and I'd call her. I said I'd come in for a wee trim, which is a laugh as if you've seen my napper, I make Bruce Willis look like Slash and just as I was leaving, her friend asked me if I'd met Machu Picchu and grabbed Martita's chest. It was a joke about her boobs being mountains due to their size and her homeland. It was a conversation full of hilarity and a bit of flirting – but little did Martita know that I was deadly serious.

So all in all, it had been another productive trip bouncing around Europe and the US but sadly I had to leave where I really wanted to be, again – and I jetted back to Australia. My emotional state had caused me to make some horrendous decisions over the previous 12 months but I did the right thing and finally shut down Pilgrim. I wanted to get it done so it wouldn't end up carrying the firm into the new financial year in Australia. It was more just a paperwork thing at that point as the business was essentially closed but I started the process of going through the legalities of terminating it and its bank accounts.

I did have Mackenzie, but Samantha had still not eased up and being so close but not being allowed to see my daughter wasn't easy either, so I felt Australia was done for me. America was where I had to be. I needed to be at the top of my sport and again selfishly, I prioritised that over everything else and I focused on it. I do feel I let my daughter down but the lure of BMX and the sport again proved too strong. But before I left there was one final bit of business I needed to attend to. And as ever with me, it involved a woman.

Doing my troubled time, I'd gotten myself into this terrible relationship where I'd been dating this woman and I really should have smelled a rat much earlier. She looked like Pamela Anderson but on one of our first dates I picked her up, we went out for lunch, and it was all going fine. Then we went back to her place and she went to the toilet. I sort of looked around as you do and noticed pictures of her wedding. It did strike me as a bit odd, bringing a new guy back and you've still got your wedding snaps up on the walls and totally innocently I asked, 'So when was your wedding?'

She said April and I immediately blurted out, 'What year?' When she said that same year, I should have sprinted off faster than Usain Bolt because this was May so she'd been married, split up and starting seeing me – all within a month. A fast mover indeed!

She had a stunning house though; it was massive with a pool room, swimming pool and a four-car garage but early into the relationship I found out she'd been married four times. I think I wanted to buy myself some affection as we'd started dating when Pilgrim fell apart and I felt pretty low. I even took her to Cancun on holiday and with my money worries, I shouldn't have been doing things like that. Then somehow she talked me into buying her a car, a Holden V8 HSV – a beast of a motor. I paid the $24,000 for it and gave her the keys but in a stroke of luck it was actually registered under my name, thank God!

And with Pilgrim shuttered and me needing cash to fund my legal application to get into the US, that $24,000 was pretty important. She ducked me originally but I finally told her, 'Either you give me the car or I get the police – as it belongs to me.' Anyway, I headed out there with my buddy Daniel 'Shift' Broman, a big dude who can handle himself, and he was my insurance policy if there was a group of guys waiting for me. Surprisingly the keys were on the front tyre like she'd finally agreed so I drove it away and we pulled over.

I grabbed some pictures on my phone and posted them immediately up on Facebook, saying I needed to sell the car instantly so it was available for $24,000. Pretty much right away, my friend Kylie messaged me saying she knew a guy who would want it and he contacted me, so I drove over to his place with the car. He actually knew my ex-girlfriend and said she'd screwed him over in the past over money too, so he wanted the car as it was a nice machine but also to stick two fingers up at her.

The only issue was he didn't have the cash immediately but he offered me a few grand less and the deal was done. Then I spotted BMX bikes in his driveway, and it turned out he was a fan of Pilgrim. So I gave him the benefit of the doubt and reduced the price due to the rush I was in. He gave me a $1,000 cash deposit then and promised to wire the balance the following day – it came through and he was a man of his word.

It was such a manic few days and Pete Robbins actually dropped me off at the airport in my own car, another Holden, but I had the SV6 station wagon. He knew I was under pressure and trying to juggle a few balls so he was going to sell my car and send me on the cash for that. That was really all I needed to do. I got whatever was owed to me and had done all the legal things by officially dissolving Pilgrim.

So after 18 years, one failed marriage, a fantastic daughter – and maybe another one too – and a hell of a lot of laughs, highs, lows and broken bones, Scottish John left Australia for the final time and headed home to Scotland.

# 13

# Here Comes Johnny

IT was refreshing to get back to my homeland where my parents were settled in, enjoying life in their new home in Monifieth and settling in comfortably to retirement. I must say that it felt a bit suffocating as I'd come from freewheeling and doing whatever I felt like to my parents wanting to look after me. It wasn't a bad thing, just that I wasn't wanting to be a teenager again, and they never got on my nerves. I understood where they were coming from totally. I did enjoy seeing them, but I was never staying.

My focus was firmly on America and as soon as I got the word about an interview for my visa I flew over to the US consulate in Belfast as I'd done a bit of research and the lines there were a lot shorter than the one in London – as there's not a consulate in Scotland.

Of course, I'd worked in a bit of female company as I'd met Annamarie, a girl from Belfast, online. She picked me up at the airport and we hung out for the weekend while I was in town. She dropped me off at the consulate and I expected that it would be much later that day when I'd be back out but it was so simple. I breezed in, went through the metal detector and security and went in for my interview.

It was all straightforward, nothing too taxing as Kelly had done his bit over in the US, so I left my passport and was told it'd either be a yes or a no. I got out and called my Belfast host and she couldn't believe it was so fast.

I also got to tick something off my bucket list as for some reason I've always wanted to have a pint of Guinness at their St James' Gate brewery in Dublin. It tastes different than anywhere else in the world; something to do with how they treat their water, although I don't know the ins and outs of it all.

So I managed to enjoy my time off. I met up with some old friends who used to work at The Angus back in the early 1990s and I went back down to Glasgow and Dundee.

Then Joe Hawk asked me to assume my international guest role again and invited me to come to Interbike in Las Vegas. I thought this might be the one year I'd miss out but I got a last-minute ticket to the party. And it wasn't just me as Joe wanted me to dust down an old idea I'd pursued in the 90s.

I'd started a website called The Generations of Freestyle, which was dedicated to the history of BMX, not just Haro – showing off all the old bikes and stories. I had cartoons on there and drawings. It was a labour of love and I just ran out of time to devote to it so I abandoned it.

But I'd told Joe about it and he wanted me to bring the idea to Vegas, so I liaised with the guys designing the show all week out there and they built a really impressive stand, coming from me describing what I'd pictured in my head. When I arrived in the hall I was gobsmacked and Mark Losey, who built it up, did a fantastic job of making this idea I'd come up with and used to doodle about with online into reality.

It was exactly what I'd dreamed of; a living and breathing BMX museum covering all the ages and Joe had agreed with me to include other brands, not just Haro. Heroes of mine like Eddie Fiola and Mike Dominguez, who I had a poster of on my wall from their visit to Livingston Skate Park in Scotland way back in 1992, handed over one of their bikes to feature. The stand had all sorts of models and colours and topping it off literally was Woody Itson's 24K gold-plated BMX, which glistened and shone brightly on top. I couldn't have wanted the idea in my brain to come to life any better.

And everyone at the show was in awe, they bloody loved it and lapped it up. It took them all from the start of BMX right up to the present day, and with the event being such a celebration there were plenty of parties going on so I was out, rubbing shoulders and trying to keep my profile up, but it wasn't easy to come crashing in at 5am and have to look lively at 8am – I didn't want Joe to see me rolling into the lobby at midday, looking like a burst couch. But I managed to keep it going and show that my professionalism wasn't in doubt.

I landed back in Scotland feeling my dream was virtually within my grasp but with plenty of time on my hands, I decided to get going with some work. I designed some parts and got in touch with a few of my old contacts out in Taiwan as I wanted to arrive in the US with ammunition and a clear plan instead of groping around in the dark.

The time seemed to fly and then my passport was back. I got a notice to collect it from a Post Office in Dundee as for some reason, they couldn't send it back to our house. So my dad gave me a lift to get it then I raced in and collected the package. I realised I was pretty much holding my future in my hands as I tore open the big padded envelope, grabbed my passport and flicked through it. And there it was. I've seen some stunning sunsets on golden beaches and been around some truly gorgeous women but that American visa was without doubt the most beautiful thing I've ever laid eyes on. I was in. I remember screaming, 'Ya fucking dancer.'

I contacted Kelly to thank him and let him know all his efforts had worked a treat, then he advised me there was one last slight technicality to tick off. I hadn't noticed, probably because I was caught up in the excitement of everything, that my passport had only a few months to run. Even though the visa entitled me to live and work in the US, Kelly said it was better to arrive with a newer passport that had longer to run so I got on the phone to the passport office and I was able to get one issued on the spot but the closest place that offered that expedited service was Glasgow.

So I went through and got it done – and that was it. Finally I was ready.

I sat down with my parents and told them it was all ready and I'd be going. They understood what a big deal it was for me as with us having such a good relationship, they knew what Haro meant to me and how BMX had become my life since I was a teenager. They remembered me going to the bakery or working extra hours in the hotel to buy brake cables from America and my dad really gushed about how he was so proud of me and that I'd followed my dream. He let slip that if he had the choice to do it all again, he'd be a professional cricket player as that was his teenage dream. A pretty big difference from being a biological scientist!

By this time it was almost Christmas and my parents wanted me to stay and celebrate it with them but I couldn't wait any longer. I'd been chewing my nails off about this opportunity and Joe had waited patiently for my visa to come through so time was of the essence so I went online that night and booked my flight to LAX – one-way of course this time around.

And I landed in my new home the United States of America on 20 December 2012. I'd made it and wee John was now leading the best and most iconic brand in BMX. I could have dropped to my knees and kissed the ground as I walked out of that airport terminal. Bring it on.

\* \* \* \* \*

I had managed to prevent myself spending Christmas on my own and had been online a lot while in Scotland, trying to make any connections or inroads over in America. Somehow I'd come across this lovely girl, Juliette Mancuso-Menunier, who was good friends with Jack Black. She picked me up at the airport and took me back to her place in Santa Monica; how's that for a blind date? We had a nice wee weekend together but then it was time to get cracking so I went down to the home of Haro's accountants Amy Lopez, and she put me up while I got my own accommodation sorted.

There was a slight anti-climax arriving on my first day as I was like a kid with ants in his pants. This was the ultimate dream for me but with it being the festive period, everything had wound down and not much was happening. So I had a week to basically settle in, set up my computer and do some admin. It was a bit frustrating as I was determined to wade in up to my armpits but looking back, it probably was a good thing as I got to find my feet.

I was glad once New Year was out of the way and everyone came back refreshed and ready to go. Well, I expected them to be. It took a few days but it wasn't long before I was sick to my stomach as more people disliked their job rather than loved it. They were moaning or complaining about this or that and they didn't seem to have any passion. I had to bite my tongue a little as I didn't want to isolate myself from all the staff but fucking hell, I knew tons of guys and girls around the world in BMX skateparks who would give their right arm to work at Haro. And I'm not kidding, a lot of them would probably do it for minimum wage – it's a privilege to be at Haro.

There's nothing that compares to it in BMX anywhere so I wasn't too happy with how the staff were conducting themselves. The place was shrouded in this negative energy and I was determined that I was going to make sure it disappeared.

I realised I not only had to kick the brand up the arse but I'd also have to use my sizes nines on the staff's backsides. I was so ashamed with the way things were being run and how the employees seemed happy with mediocrity. I didn't put a Haro sticker on my car for the first 12 months in the US as I didn't want to be associated with the bang average way we were going about things. I wasn't going to fly the flag that I was part of a rudderless ship and it got to the point where I had to give a few people a bit of the hairdryer treatment. For anyone who's not heard of that, it's a bit of a Scottish speciality done by football managers – you get in the person's face and give them a blast.

I ended up saying to a few startled people, 'Look, if you don't love your job here, then fuck off, you're wasting my time and your own time.'

And while I could work on the attitudes around the place, I needed to get the product back to the top immediately. Haro was basically producing boring, generic bikes that no one really liked and more importantly, no one really wanted to ride. Some people might have bought them just because it was a Haro and the name obviously meant something but it wasn't them looking at magazines or YouTube videos and really wanting to ride one of our machines.

In BMX manufacturing there's a thing called the Taiwan Buyers' Guide. It's a catalogue of all the parts that you can get made in Taiwanese factories, and there's pages and pages of things. There's nothing wrong with it and a lot of smaller companies use it to make their bikes but I couldn't believe Haro was doing the same.

The most prestigious brand on the planet was sitting there in America, ticking a few pages of pre-made parts and then just putting a Haro sticker on them. There was no way that was going to be continuing on my watch, although I was going to continue with Taiwan, as that's where the better bikes are made. So it's not a case of the TBG being poor standard, it's just that things are generic.

The cheap bikes are made in China but very few big companies go there now as because of anti-dumping laws in the EU you have to add a 48 per cent tax on to Chinese bikes, which is something I've never understood. There's no such tax on things like iPhones or laptops, so why on bikes? Anyway, that ruled out China due to the price point.

Bangladesh is where your cheap shit is made, it's really low quality stuff – but it's not Haro and no bikes are made in the US or UK anymore.

It's a nice idea to made all of your own parts but the cost involved means it's just not feasible. A welder working on BMX parts would earn ten times more in America but over in China or Taiwan, you're looking at way below a minimum-wage income and if you're trying to sell an entry-level bike for $199, there's no way you can contemplate changing the current production model.

So Taiwan was fine but this generic picking of parts was a thing of the past. I got on to my connections over there and told them, 'Look, we're coming back at Haro,' and I began designing our own parts. I sketched out rims, cranks and stems. I wanted personality and passion, and I wanted someone to cruise by on one, so that kids were swivelling their heads to check out the flash bike.

I didn't have a name or marketing plan to get this over to the general public. It's like my car, I drive a Chevrolet Camaro. It's the 2010 model and why do I love it? It looks like the big iconic American muscle cars from the 1960s but it's a modern motor with all the technology, and you could still imagine Starksy and Hutch springing out of it. The show was actually going to use the Camaro but a last-minute switch saw them actually use the now classic Ford Gran Torino. So that's where my head was.

Serendipitously, just as I was doing this, I happened to be having a quick bite to eat with Dennis McCoy. We were shooting the breeze at Subway and I told him what I was doing and how I wanted to change things. He nodded along and then said, 'It's like that Lineage idea I proposed.' I asked back, 'What idea was that?' It turned out that Dennis had gone into Haro and made a pitch to design a range of bikes, along the same lines as I wanted to. But some bright spark in the office had filed the paperwork in the shredder and it never saw the light of day.

But as soon as I heard the word Lineage over our 12-inchers – that was it. I knew that was my key identifier right there and I'm keen that Dennis gets all the credit for it – he came up with it.

I thundered into the office the following Monday morning and asked Joe about why Lineage didn't get taken up but he'd never heard of it, no one had passed it along. Well, better late than never. And it was going to be done now.

Lineage was going to be how we catered for the serious riders as they'd appreciate what we were trying to do, but I also had to think as not everyone was going to have had pictures of Mike Dominguez and Brian Blyther up on their bedroom walls. I wanted to drag more and more kids into our wonderful sport so I pondered over how we could get them interested and get them to try their hand.

It might not be for everyone but I will argue with anyone until I'm blue in the face that BMX is a fun, exciting and challenging sport that cuts across gender and ethnic differences. But I couldn't see how Haro was ever going to excite any youngsters with the then models being the 100, 200, 300, 400 and 500. For Christ's sake, you'd hesitate to call commercial photocopier models such boring names. And here we were, selling what was supposed to be one of the most fun things ever calling them that?

Remember, virtually every kid's first bike is a BMX, as they've got no gears and are the best way to learn how to ride. I thought back to my own childhood and what my BMX meant to me all those years ago standing in Dales with my parents and choosing my all-chrome Piranha XL. I went for that because it got my heart pumping and then it gave me freedom. I was master of my own domain, I could go anywhere and do my own thing, so I applied that literally. That's how I devised our advertising slogan – 'Where will your bike take you? Where will your passion take you?'

Then our team designed the bikes, again using some of our own parts, and due to cost, they couldn't be quite as intricate as the Lineage models were but we still made them look sharp and put the same amount of passion into them. The days of phoning in orders from a catalogue were over.

We started with the Downtown – as every city has an area called that, so any kid could think of going there on their bike. It wasn't meant to be complicated, it was simple. I wanted the world to know that Haro was going to make legitimate BMX bikes and you could take them anywhere. The other models were Boulevard, Midway, Interstate and Plaza and top of the range was the SD (San Diego), as that was where BMX began back in the late 1960s. The SD was also Dennis Enarson's signature model. And as a nice twist of fate, it was exactly what had happened to me as my bike had taken me to San Diego – eventually.

So I wanted other kids to know that their bike could take them to the top of our sport – and also it could inspire them to reach other goals in their lives. It didn't have to literally be coming out to the birthplace of BMX like I had, it was about showing what dedication and passion can do for your life. I pushed the vendors to keep the prices as low as they could and squeezed the factories in Taiwan to do what they could for us too on cost.

I was determined that I was going to zap the BMX world with a bolt of lighting. That was Lineage. Our plan was for every top rider to want to be back on a Haro, and at the same time give every kid out there the chance to ride a bike that would be fun and offer them a way to think big and dream, just like BMX had done for me.

I gritted my teeth and knew it wasn't going to be easy but I had spent months on end in Broughty Ferry as a wee guy learning how to pull off an abubaca and this was exactly the same, I would keep trying for as long as it took to get it right. I can't pretend that the reaction to my ideas and blueprint for Haro has not gone down a bomb, although some might say that's me being arrogant or patting myself on the back.

Nothing could be further from the truth and I've been humbled by the reaction as over the last few years I've had a stack of letters, e-mails and Instagram messages from the great and the good.

But the best buzz has been when your normal Joe Bloggs has reached out to me. Not long before I wrote this, a deaf chap got in touch and his speech was hard to understand, but he persevered and told me how amazing the new range has been.

People are now seeing what I always saw, that Haro is head and shoulders above all the other brands. And the best bit, there's no magic formula or black arts – all we had to do was be Haro. The people making the decisions before me couldn't see the forest for the trees in some ways. Joe has been really complimentary and I'm particularly pleased to have repaid his faith in me. He waited and pleaded my case with the shareholders in Taiwan, so it makes me feel good that I've delivered the goods and I don't give a fuck if anyone thinks it's not appropriate to say it – but yeah, I have turned the ship around. I've steered us away from the icebergs and now we're sailing on the high seas which in business terms translates to between a seven and a nine per cent average increase in our sales year on year.

That's no mean feat as the BMX market is actually shrinking in the mainstream with quite a few of the dedicated stores having gone bust and big chains are not buying as many. So it's even more impressive that we're growing and getting bigger but I haven't rested on my laurels. Once I'd got the bikes sorted out, I turned my attention to our riders and this was the much easier part of the task, as I'm a rider myself.

So it's not something I really had to think about but like the Haro bikes, the team needed freshening up – they were dynamic but there was just something missing. What was I looking for?

I wanted riders who could do it on and off the bike. First were our two US Olympians, Nic Long and Brooke Crain, and even though I didn't recruit them I encouraged them to always respect the kids like they respect you, as they're the future of our sport and the ones who will keep it going. So if someone wants a picture, or asks them a question on Twitter – I expect them to do it.

It shows what Haro is all about; we're classy and we're in this sport for all the right reasons. No one is shunned or made to feel they can't fit in. Yes, Nic and Brooke can do things that 90 per cent of young riders will never be able to, but that's not their role at Haro. I want them to win medals and contests in all four corners of the globe but also to carry that Haro name with pride and always remember that they're part of something bigger. Take me; I started off in this sport, sitting in a cinema watching Bob Haro riding in *ET*, so they could have that same impact with any kid they come into contact with.

I want parents also to think, 'it's a brand that we want our kids to be riding' and I'm always mindful that we're also representing the sport as a whole. But we're not just about projecting an image and doing well for the kids, I want us to have the best pro riders and give them the best bikes to ride. I also have a few Olympians from Japan and Germany plus at the 2016 Games in Rio, I had to pause the TV as I noticed a South African rider on a Haro. And we don't even pay him. If you're reading, pal, thanks for the free advertising!

The freestyle team are really on another level. Those riders really touch the BMX community and go deep into their hearts – and I've changed that root and branch. We kept Dennis Enarson, a class operator who won gold at the 2016 summer X Games. I really like how he rides and that's why we put out his own signature frame.

Chad Kerley, this slick, cool young dude, signed with us before I arrived. He's laid-back and is a very warm person. I couldn't think of anyone better to carry the Haro brand.

We've also got Ryan Nyquist, Haro's second-longest-serving employee after Joe Hawk. He's been on the team for 20 years now and quite simply, he's a legend. I don't see a day when Ryan isn't riding a Haro as he's quite simply a BMX icon.

The others are riders that I've found myself. Mike Gray is our Canadian guy who I'd seen online, and watching his videos I was going, 'Damn, this lad has it in spades.'

He has really good skills and can get you up on your feet but I would never have signed him until we met; I'd already done my research – and he didn't let me down. Mike is a proper fella and I was happy to stand by him.

Then I was at Dennis Enarson's house for a lunch one day and I was introduced to Tyler Fernengel. He was a young guy and I'd spotted him the previous year at the Texas Toast contest in Austin with this glint in his eye that screamed that he would go for anything, so we offered him a deal not long after that lunch. Tyler has also teamed up with Red Bull and did the iconic display in the abandoned Silverdome in Pontiac, Michigan – he's from Detroit, which isn't too far away, so it had a nice local connection as he did all sorts of crazy stunts in that desolate concrete jungle. Tyler fitted ideally with my younger, fresher approach – he wasn't jaded or expecting any handouts and he was hungry which has helped drive the other riders on at Haro, keeping them on their toes.

The other young guy we wanted and finally got is the French superstar Matthias Dandois. He doesn't do any air jumps or high-octane stuff – he's what we call a flatlander, meaning everything is done on the ground, but he is a ballerina on a bike, which is how I describe him to anyone who doesn't know him. He's a real specialist but has honed his craft to a fine degree. I admire his passion and dedication to do one thing, but to do it better than anyone else.

Still though, I didn't offer him a deal until we met and what sealed it was his smile. He's always smiling, which I love as that's what I want. It's a great way to spend your life, being on a BMX and travelling the world, and if you're getting paid then you should be grinning like a Cheshire cat. Young, old, white, black, male, female, everyone can relate to that. They see Matthias and instantly their brain says 'BMX looks like it's a lot of fun' and Haro is right in there providing that fun.

I also dipped back to my Forgotten days to sign up Australian rider Jason Watts. I've known him for many years and knew he needed a bigger platform so we brought him over to America to join us, and I'm sure my ex-partners loved that! He was the one thing about Forgotten that I didn't erase from my memory.

I'll back all my riders in the same way as back in my earlier days I wouldn't sell anything I wouldn't ride myself. I'd never sign a rider to Haro that I wouldn't call a friend and vouch for and they know that, as does our team manager Colin MacKay, who is a consummate professional.

They were also key to me expanding the brand and my idea of 'Where will your bike take you? Where will your passion take you?'

So I opted to use our global team as they are all Haro, but they're from all different parts of the world. I thought we should use that and show Haro to everyone in these places. I got Matthias to do a photo shoot at the Eiffel Tower as it's one place that everyone recognises. The subtle link I wanted to create was that no matter where you are, you'll recognise a Haro too. Next up was Jason's shoot at the Sydney Opera House and Cam Pianta, an old Pilgrim rider of mine, took the photos that day in another nice coincidence.

One of our British riders, Simon Tabron, who is from Liverpool but came to the US with me, went to London – and I told him to do a surfer, which is standing on the handlebars and frame. Then we shot Simon as he did that cruising across Abbey Road, at the famous pelican crossing from the Beatles' album cover and then outside the Houses of Parliament.

Mike Gary did his in Toronto, where we used the CN Tower and the iconic view there. Dennis of course did the San Diego shoot, as it's where Haro is from and also where he was raised. So he was the perfect guy with the looks and moves like a BMXer. We used the USS *Midway* aircraft carrier for Dennis as it's now docked there as a tourist attraction.

None of these shoots were crude ways to just sell more bikes. For me it was about showing anyone who didn't know what BMX was all about. It's fun and it's worldwide. You can do it in all sorts of weird and wonderful places, and vitally, you can have fun doing it.

That's what I wanted to convey and I think I did that as all of my ideas and concepts are part of the reason Haro is back on top. The riders have played their part too; there is so much love and passion from the staff at Haro also.

We've all come together as one and really brought the magic back.

# 14

# Celebrity Connections

O NE of the most fun parts of the job has been getting to know different fans of Haro. Most of the people who actually end up speaking to me are celebrities, and it's really surprising the weird and wonderful characters that are into BMX.

One huge fan is Blink 182 guitarist Matt Skiba, who got in touch as he wanted some Haro Freestyler stickers so his Gibson guitar could identically match his green 1986 Haro Master. If you've seen them on their world tour and wondered where the garish colour scheme came from – it's my fault! Matt actually bought his bike, which is not really the norm as most celebrities get them free as a perk.

It's not about trying to impress them or get them to like Haro. I only do it when they get in touch, so I already know they're BMXers, but it's great marketing especially in today's world of social media.

We sorted out a bike for the rapper Meek Mill and I also got one dispatched to the rock band Rancid's drummer Branden Steineckert, who is such a big rider that he was telling me about the mini-ramp he had built in his back garden.

Carey Hart is also right into our bikes. I've mentioned him before as we'd crossed paths at Planet X over in New Zealand many years ago. As he's married the pop singer Pink he has become a seriously big name in the tabloids but all of us in the extreme sports world already knew him as a talented operator – he was the first guy to do a backflip on a motorbike. Before Carey the engines kept conking out and it couldn't be done.

Rarely does anyone in the action sports world get too big for their boots and Carey is the same. He reached out as he wanted a bike for his daughter Willow and I wasn't in the US at the time, but I told him I'd get back to him. It was for her birthday so I sent it over as a gift from Haro – and he even graciously posted a picture of Willow on it on his Instagram, and Haro never says no to that kind of endorsement!

Someone a long time ago called me a chameleon and I think there's something in that. I do find it quite natural interacting with different people; it could be a kid in a skatepark, high-powered business gurus or celebrities – I treat everyone the same. Particularly when you're dealing with big names, if you act like you're a fan and fawn around them then they treat you like a pleb. Plus BMX is my domain and I don't ever fear being out of my depth. The one time I've felt that was right back at the beginning when I first came across Scott Carroll.

The celebrity calls are another sign to me that what I've done has worked. It cuts through all the other crap and hits home as these sort of people have the means to get usually pretty much anything they want within reason. So to have them calling asking for a Haro means we've touched their worlds.

I feel the brand is in superb shape top to bottom as I've targeted and successfully managed to hit each of my aims. We're genuinely back as the BMX kings and no matter who you are, you realise that.

And that's become an issue for me as I feel like a soldier who was sent out into the field with a mission – and that mission is virtually completed. I can't go anywhere from here, I've nowhere to go in Haro and all my life I've been on a journey to better myself and achieve in BMX. And now I've done that at Haro; I've loved them, I've collected them, I've ridden them, I've designed them, I've managed them.

Before I may have been happy to tread water but in 2011, I really took my old buddy Paul Everest's slogan from his Unit Clothing – 'One Life, One Chance' – to heart after breaking my neck.

Now I've done it.

I'm almost at the stage where I'll be in cruise control and that can't work for me. I'm a born fighter who needs the fire inside me to be raging – that's when I'm at my best. But that's not to say riding is over for me. Not at all, I still ride and have a blowout on the ramps if I've got time outside of my Haro duties.

There are plenty of other avenues that I could go down with BMX and I do get asked quite often if there's any future for the sport. And of course there is. It's a different world from when I was a kid in the 1980s but it's a different world for all sports. The internet, computers, smartphones and all of the resulting things that have come from that sphere now dominate for kids. But there are still plenty of people lining up to play in the NBA and there's no shortage of footballers signing deals with Manchester United or Real Madrid. And BMX is the same.

The riders now have hundreds of thousands and sometimes millions of followers on their Twitter or Instagram accounts, so clearly it's still alive and well, and in some ways I think it might even have more of an attraction as BMX is as analogue as it can get.

It's you and your bike – nothing else. I feel kids will actually relish that more than previous generations did as it's a very hard sensation to experience today – it may even be a new sensation for lots of them. And with modern technology and ideas, we can do loads of stunts that grab attention, whether it's Robbie Maddison riding a motorbike on the water or Jed Mildon somersaulting through the air.

So for me, BMX is going nowhere – it does and will always have a place. It's an established sport that gives so much as a participant and as a spectator. You can't be thrilled in many ways like you can perched on the saddle of a BMX and gripping the handlebars for dear life. BMX is a titan and it's standing tall but what my part in that will be in the years to come, who knows?

# 15

# Bob Haro

DESPITE it seeming like my input at Haro has been universally liked, one key player is not in that camp – well, that's how it feels to me and while I can't talk for him, this is just my opinion. That man is Bob Haro.

You might be surprised to find that out and I don't want to confuse things or deliver a bout of hyperbole. We're not enemies, we're actually good pals and if we're in the same room, we can be perfectly civil and not resort to throwing bowls of fruit at each other.

I'd met Bob twice before I joined Haro and I was pretty impressed with his aura. I had also e-mailed him before that, when I had Pilgrim, but he'd ignored me. I did, however, know the Australian rider Steve Cassap as we had struck up a friendship while I was over there. He told Bob about me and what I was doing in the sport, so Bob then replied to my e-mails.

It was still a real buzz to meet Bob for the first time and I told him 'you saved my life' as BMX really has been my way out of all my problems, it's given me a purpose. I don't know if I'd ever have found it without watching *ET*. Maybe I would but as they say, if your uncle was a woman called Judy, he'd be your auntie. So Bob and I know each other but we're not close and never have been. I wouldn't say I could ever imagine us going on holiday, although we have had a few laughs down the years together.

But I have the utmost respect for Bob. He started this brand that I've been obsessed with and loved for the last 35 years and he even said so in the letter he wrote about me to the US government, which helped me land my visa. So I am happy to admit that I owe a debt to Bob and would never wish to take anything away from what he's achieved.

With that said, I can't lie that I've not been massively disappointed in him recently as we're flying with the Lineage range, the young riders, sales are up, and everyone is excited again by Haro – but to me Bob has become a little bitter. A few times I've asked him if he'd maybe do a few little things for us, as the company obviously carries his name. He refuses unless there's payment involved and I wouldn't mind covering his expenses or sorting out travel or whatever it may be.

It's just the message I get that he's no longer in love with the brand like I am and he isn't pleased about how well we're doing. But in some ways I get that, it's a bit like – how often do you want to see your ex-wife?

I've also heard little whispers on the grapevine – that could be false – that he resents my idea of using his old classic bikes as the blueprint for our current ones. I don't know if that's because we're reaching a level that he hasn't in a long time or maybe it's because he's jealous about no longer owning Haro. I do find it strange that he's not gushing and over the moon with how things are doing.

To me, surely it's only a good thing that the brand he created and carries his name is performing as well as it possibly could. But whenever I find myself around him now, I sort of feel a slight chill in the air. Like I said, it's nothing aggressive but there's just this feeling that he doesn't want to see me doing what I'm doing now. I try not to think about it too much as it's not easy when one of your heroes isn't in your camp.

While at Haro, I've also quite literally put my money – or some of my own money – where my mouth was. Not many people know this but I tried to buy Haro as I wanted to return the company all the way to its original beginnings, back to American ownership. It's not some anti-foreigner thing as I'm Scottish myself, so it's not me being hypocritical. But I wanted to return Haro to where it started and in a bid to do that in 2015, I offered the shareholders in Taiwan $20m to sell up. It was a pretty good price as I went through the books myself and I also got some professional opinion on the company too, so it was an attractive amount. Where was I getting a wedge like that?

Through my old mucker Andrea Piana. It was a sweet turn of events that he was providing the finance as we'd actually met because of Haro – all those years ago back in Dundee. We lost touch but once Facebook became popular, we found each other and now both live in America. I knew that the Piana family had a textile business as Andrea had mentioned that his dad and uncle have factories in different cities. So it took me by surprise when I read that LMVH, who own Louis Vuitton, Dior and Moët & Chandon, bought the company Loro Piana for about $2bn.

Anyway, Andrea had access to serious funds so when he heard about my idea to buy Haro he offered to lend me the cash and the deal was I'd repay it within five years, which I was confident I could do.

I also had other investors who had seen what I'd done as global brand manager and reckoned I could do even more with ownership. But the shareholders refused, even though it was a good deal for them; they just weren't interested. The shutters were pulled down and I had to accept the decision. It's completely their right to sell if they wish – and they don't. I've made my peace with it and Haro is something I'll never plan to turn my back on.

But there's one ambition that has sprung up like an itch that I need to scratch. I've got the bug to get into Hollywood. I'm a shit actor, I know that all too well from my Australian TV endeavours, but I think I've got the minerals to crack the world of voiceovers. That's huge right now as movies like *Lego Batman*, *Toy Story*, *Minions* and *Kung Fu Panda* are a seriously big deal and I don't know what it is, but I fancy a crack at a bit of that – or even playing some zany characters like Austin Powers and Fat Bastard, as I love putting on an accent and having fun with it.

Everything in life that I've set out to achieve – I have. And I don't feel any different about this. It would be a lovely little addition to my life and now I've seen the film business from the inside out – I want more. So you might be hearing more of me down the line.

# 16

# The Drugs Don't Work

THE bad part for the old BMX dinosaurs like myself is that we're riddled with pain, and that's hardly a surprise. We've used our bodies like crash test dummies for decades, and while it's amusing and interesting to hear about all our injuries there's a darker side to it.

Dave Mirra is a well-known example of someone who took his own life, and my ultimate BMX idol Scott Carroll succumbed too and committed suicide in 1998. Even then I still looked up to him and when I got the message from friends telling me the news, I went numb. I've still not come to terms with it and lots of BMXers have gone down a similar route.

The problem is twofold. Firstly, we're adrenaline junkies, which is par for the course in the action sports world – and BMX is no different. You're used to doing all sorts of hair-raising things on the bike. And then when you retire it's gone. There's no weaning off, it's bang, over – cold turkey and you're left with this massive void to fill. It's impossible to replace that in normal life as you just don't get those surges of energy going to the shopping mall or meeting your partner for lunch.

That's not to say normal life is boring but it's just that riding is a feeling like no other. I know that better than most as I chose BMX over my marriage and I left my daughter behind in Australia to thrive in the sport but others maybe don't have the avenues available that I did to replace a lot of the on-the-bike action. So they might start taking drugs, or drinking heavily and from there, they might slip into depression and their life can unravel pretty quickly.

If it can happen to Dave, then it can happen to anyone – he had everything you could want in life from a material point of view but all the money in the world couldn't replace the thrill of doing what he loved. It's just a shame it ended that way for Dave as he was a legend who deserved to bask in the legacy he'd created. But there are countless others, not so well known, who have met with a similar demise. Suicide is tragically the only option for a lot of riders as they finally succumb to being unable to replace the buzz of doing what they've loved all their days.

The second issue, which is arguably bigger, is prescription drugs as our bodies have soaked up a lot of punishment – and it's not easy to live with. My knees ache like crazy if I sit in a certain position but other riders have issues with their legs, ankles, elbows, necks, backs – you name it, we've broken it. And then broken it again.

As these injuries are so serious you never really get over them totally. In our day there wasn't sophisticated sport science whereas if one of my Haro US Olympians broke a bone, they would get physio and have an intensive rehab programme laid out in order to get the bone to be as strong as it was, if not stronger, so they could ride again. Whereas we'd be riding with bones sticking out of our shins just to complete the contest. No one wanted to limp off – and never before you'd pulled off the jump you'd come to do.

Look at my old pal Stephen Murray, who lost it on a double backflip and ended up a quadriplegic, although he is not bitter at all or regretful about taking on that jump. Neither am I about breaking my neck in 2011. I couldn't have had another try that day as I was unable to stand but I eventually went back risking it happening again to do the jump – that was important to me. I couldn't give a shit if I won a gold medal, it was about nailing that jump. That is worth more than any award you can be given. Even if I had snapped my neck again, I'd have gone back for a third bash.

So while we might appear to be superhuman, we're not. The pain eventually catches up with you and you're struggling. I used to be on prescription painkillers every day and I wasn't addicted, but I'd take them to just help me move about more freely. I also used to sometimes smoke weed as it mellowed out the pain in the same way but as soon as I heard about Dave, I flushed all my pain meds down the toilet and vowed to never go back to using things like that as a crutch.

But so many other riders are really in deep shit and doctors seem happy to write out prescriptions ten a penny, and they end up depending on these pills. After you're used to having it numbed, when the pain comes back at full strength you notice it more and it seriously disrupts your equilibrium – it's a question of tolerance.

There's lots of talk nowadays about concussion and Chronic Traumatic Encephalopathy (CTE), which is a brain disease that's being linked to the after-effects on absorbing and taking impact. I have my own views on how valid that is, but I understand doctors and researchers have their place. However, I don't think CTE is as big an issue as the one where all these athletes are popping painkillers like they're jelly beans. It screws a lot of us up and has knock-on effects into their families and personal relationships. I really do feel that retired riders are forgotten about and not enough attention is given to this.

Drugs are part of BMX though and I'd say that about 50 per cent of pro freestyle riders smoke weed. I'm not talking about your Olympians and those sort of people – they are consummate professionals but within freestylers, the ones doing the big jumps and stunts, it's very common. I've done it myself throughout my life, and although I wasn't massively into drugs in the BMX scene you get exposed to people passing around joints. And then before you know it, you're smoking a bit.

Again it comes back to the pain issue, as we've all heard about weed's ability to mellow things and dull the sensations. For practical reasons it seems logical to see why it's so common but it's also just part of the culture. Harder drugs sometimes do creep in, but it's not like you'd see riders shooting up heroin before jumping on the bike. It's a ride hard, party hard sort of scene.

So you end up at clubs and big bashes, lots of the people around you don't have many inhibitions, and things are tried. I've done plenty myself, not to ride, but you do come across it in the BMX world.

I've also come into contact with it in my personal life. I was actually back in Scotland a few months prior to writing this book and I had a line or two of cocaine during a night out in my old stomping ground of Dundee. I first got into messing around with substances because I couldn't ride thanks to the notoriously wet Scottish climate. Some days even I had to admit defeat and ended up doing speed and dropping acid. I was never addicted or needed it – it was more a social thing to do while I was off the bike.

Now I'm in no way endorsing drugs or encouraging anyone to do them and I'd be livid if I saw any of our Haro riders doing them at one of our events or while riding our bikes. What they do in their free personal time is none of my business but when they're on the Haro clock, we are very anti-drugs and rightly so. If I saw it going down or being promoted, they'd be off the team.

I might have done drugs but it doesn't mean I think kids should be doing them. I just wanted to own up and say it like it was, rather than patronising youngsters by saying I've never done anything like that, when they know fine well that lots of us have.

The weed issue is a different matter as the real hardcore BMXers don't see it as any different than having a beer or a glass of wine. Everyone has their own views and boundaries on those type of things but there's never been an inkling that smoking a joint makes you a better rider.

BMX is not pro-drugs. That's a lazy stereotype which has no real merit and it's almost like a vicious cycle that to earn your stripes and be a real freestyle rider, you need to pull off the daring jumps and tricks. When you do, unless you're going down the structured and sheltered route, you're eventually going to get hurt. And when you do, it's highly likely to be serious; broken bones are a certainty. So prescription painkillers and smoking weed are a result of that and they give you the ability to keep doing what you love – which causes more injuries. It's a hamster wheel.

But it doesn't have to be. It's all down to personal choice as BMX is a pure sport and really is about being high on life. Anything on top of that is down to external factors and with a bit more care and attention, we could eradicate most of the traps so less and less riders end up in dire times – and even less take the ultimate final step like Mirra.

I bizarrely found out about Dave via my hometown Glasgow. Nitro Circus was on a worldwide tour and stopped there that night as the athletes in it used to ride for me and we're all mates, so Matt Whyatt called me to let me know as some of the guys there had been contacted by Dave's family. I respected Dave but I wasn't in awe of him. I had made a good name for myself and worked hard on my skills so with Dave, he was just another rider and that's how he wanted to be treated as he was sick of having the red carpet rolled out and being treated like a VIP. He was never that kind of guy; he was down to earth.

I actually contacted Dave on the day he died. We had become close friends as by then, I was out in America. Anyway, a few days before his death I'd texted him as I wanted to meet up at an old school reunion at Woodward Camp in Pennsylvania and go for a ride. We'd done a lot together but had never actually got on the bikes and went on a ramp for a laugh. He replied saying, 'John, it would be a privilege to ride with you.'

Then on the day he died, 4 February 2016, I texted him again but the exact details actually send a chill down my spine. I sent a text from California at 4pm – something inside just told me to reach out. I was worried about him, and my message was, 'Dave, are you OK mate?' I've still got the messages on my phone.

It has since transpired that Dave killed himself at 4pm in North Carolina. So I sent mine at exactly the same time, just in a different time zone – I can't get that out of my head.

It was such a shame to lose a legend of our sport but unfortunately it's more common than people think. BMX puts you on the edge and some people seem to tip over.

I don't know why Dave killed himself. It's not for me to speculate or delve into his personal business but there has been a lot said about CTE – and it's been linked to Dave since his death. It's flagged up all the time and I'll just say, I don't buy that it's as big a part of BMX as what a lot of so-called experts claim.

I must add though it's been an honour to help Dave's legacy live on as at Haro we did a deal to license Dave's name and launched a range of bikes dedicated to him. We did this gorgeous candy red bike with chrome parts, which is modelled on the bike that Dave is riding on the cover of his PlayStation game from 2000. And a large percentage of the money earned is being given to a fund that will help hard-up youngsters get the chance to experience BMX and hopefully give them some fun and enjoyment – and maybe inspire a few to become professionals like Dave down the line.

If you want to get involved or find out more, go to www.davemirra.com.

# 17

# Landmark

AMERICA has also sparked a turnaround in my personal fortunes. I've actually got together with the woman who I'd describe as the love of my life, the delightfully named Martita Gastiaburu. We'd met during my time over in San Diego as an international guest of Haro and when I finally made it on to US soil, I called just like I said I would. And we hit it off, began dating and it felt great, so a year or so later we moved in together.

I had never experienced anything like it. I shared everything about myself and so did she. I never had that with Samantha, and Martita also introduced me to the Landmark programme. It's a motivational therapy scheme where you go along to meetings and share experiences, while listening and learning from the instructor. You're wearing name badges and on the surface it's all very cliched and inside about five minutes,

I thought everybody in the room was a bloody weirdo; I couldn't believe they were eating up this crap.

At the intermission I shouted that it was all rubbish and I stormed out – with an embarrassed Martita chasing after me. I think it was the idea of being controlled or made to conform that sent me spinning, almost like I was back in Glenrosa Children's Home. I ripped off my badge and had my hand on my car door when I stopped. 'Do you think they'll let me back in?' I had this feeling inside that despite my emotional response, there was something in it. So there I was, this confident, loud, extrovert BMXer appearing back with his tail firmly between his legs.

Fair play to all the people in the room, they didn't bat an eyelid and let me join back in so I started listening to the rest of the session and it really connected. I signed up for the 12-week programme and learned it's all about living a life of integrity and living the life you love. Landmark taught me that if you've made a mistake, the best thing to do is confront it. Admit it and then put it out of your mind as you can't affect the past – and that's really plagued me all my days.

From my childhood horrors to the guilt of initially treating my parents badly when I first moved into their home and then the way I chewed myself inside out over my adultery; it's not about saying I wasn't to blame or didn't make mistakes but Landmark has taught me to deal with them and move on.

Also a key part of that deals with living in the moment. You could be on a golden beach, sipping a pina colada as crystal clear water laps at your feet, but your mind is on flying back to your normal life the following day. You start worrying and dread going back to the day job – but what's the point? You have to live in the moment, that's something I've really begun doing since my accident in 2011 when I broke my neck, and Landmark crystallised it all for me.

They also teach you a crazy set of phrases that sound bonkers, but when you let them digest – it's deep. You know what you know so you know how to make a cup of tea or drive a car. You know what you don't know, so we know we can't fly or breathe underwater. But you don't know what you don't know. There are so many things out there that we can't think about as they don't touch us – unless you embrace life and take it in, you'll miss them. I've really found it an amazing help and it's given me some badly needed balance to my personal life.

Even better, I got to share it with Martita. We had a great three years together but it came to an end at Christmas 2015. Sadly, I cheated. I had an affair with a woman who I won't name – purely for the simple reason that she's married and is now back with her husband and I don't want to rain on their parade.

When I went through trauma with my wife, I bottled it up and let it destroy our marriage. This time I just told Martita what was happening. It didn't make me feel good and I wasn't stupid enough to think I had done her a favour but at least I'd grown to the point I could properly admit what I'd done wrong or what I was feeling. And we stayed together. It obviously hurt her but I gave her all the details – and we moved on. I think the one grain of comfort she could take was that if I was ever going to do that, I'd at least always tell her.

I took Martita over to Scotland to let her see where I was from and she vowed that for her 50th birthday – she's older than me – she would take me to her homeland, Peru, but when it came around she suggested we postpone until Christmas as money was tight. I was completely understanding as I wasn't expecting my partner to pay for fancy holidays and when Christmas came, it was the same story; she called it off again due to the cost. Then shortly after I saw her son driving about in a new car that his hard-working mum bought him. I blew my lid and I went purple with rage – I couldn't stomach it.

I feel Martita was enabling him so I had to cut my cloth and I left her but I still regret it in some ways as we had a great thing.

We're still close and she's my best friend in the world but just since adopting my one life, one chance mindset and doing Landmark, I can't settle or paper over the cracks. It's got to be right and I'm hyper-aware that I'm only here for a certain period and I've got to be honest with myself first and foremost – and then everyone else of course.

I did feel vindicated though not long after when Martita told me her son's car had broken down and she'd gone to help him out. At the time, the charity jar had gone missing. It was just something we'd started to throw coins in now and then, and at Christmas time we would give it to the homeless. It was our way of giving something back. Anyway, it went missing and then a short while after, when she turned up to help him out, Martita spotted it in the back seat of his car. It gave me no pleasure to know I'd been right but at least I knew I'd done what I thought was best.

# 18

# Hollywood

THE latest episode in my American sojourn has surprised even me as my life has been turned into a Hollywood movie. Yes, that wee John from Whiteinch has somehow ended up on the silver screen. I still have to pinch myself that it's actually happened.

Even Tony Hawk knows about it as we ended up sitting next to each other on a plane and he brought it up – and he's the most famous action sports star alive.

A couple of years ago I was sitting at my desk and the phone rang. The guy on the other end of the line introduced himself as Ali Afshar and he knew a contact of mine, Miles Rogoish, who has filmed for us a few times at Haro. He had given Ali my details and Ali explained how much of a BMX fan he was and he loved our new Mike Dominguez signature bike. It's pretty common that I get these kind of calls but I was polite enough and palmed him off to my sales manager. Later on, I heard Ali bought eight bikes, one in each of the different colours – so I knew he was into the sport.

Fast forward 12 months. My phone goes and it's Ali again. He's asking me, 'Why didn't you call?' It took a minute for my brain to click into gear and remember him – and I asked, 'Call you about what, mate?' He instantly came back telling me we'd done the Brian Blyther signature bike and hadn't let him know but we'd let the world know via press releases and plastered pictures all over the internet. Anyway, Ali asked if he could drive over and buy it now. I told him that wasn't a problem – it was nice to see a fan with some genuine enthusiasm.

For some reason I decided to Google Ali. He had mentioned that he was a Hollywood movie producer and you hear a lot of stuff from people moving in the circles I do – but he was straight up. I saw he'd been in *Three Kings*, which starred George Clooney and Mark Wahlberg – and also *Godzilla* too. And he's produced quite a few films, so in a nutshell he was legit.

Two hours later he appeared at Haro and came into my office so we got him a bike and he asked to take me out to lunch. I was a bit reluctant as I had a lot on that day but I liked his spirit and off we went. Ali told me about himself, how he'd been a racing driver and had the world's fastest Subaru. That's a fact, check it out online – it's a beast and has something like 1,600 brake horsepower.

Then we got on to me, as you do during a chat. Ali is a really easy guy to talk to and we ended up getting into my days back in Glasgow, me being thrown in a fire at three, living on the streets and the children's home, then my adoption and all the rest. Just as we were finishing, he blurted out that not only did he *want* to – he was actually *going* to make my movie. I remember almost rolling my eyes, thinking, 'Yeah, sure you are, buddy.'

We kept in touch as friends but every so often Ali would bring up this notion of the John Buultjens movie. I really thought it was never going to happen and the only time I actually believed that it was a serious proposition was when a contract arrived. I was looking at it and reading it, expecting some film crew to pop out from behind a pillar and reveal that I was in an episode of *America's Most Gullible Idiots*. I had to get myself a lawyer and thankfully I'd met a nice guy, Chris Scott-Dixon at Landmark, who was an attorney as they say over here. So he looked it all over for me and gave me the green light and I put my signature on the contract, still sort of wondering what the hell this was going to lead to.

I then went through a series of long conversations with scriptwriters, who grilled me on my life. It was along the lines of me reading this book out loud to them but they selected certain incidents that jumped out as ideal movie scenes. This all took about 18 months, from when Ali took me out for lunch. I was still expecting it all to fizzle out and for the script to be left in someone's filing cabinet in Hollywood gathering dust for years on end.

You could have knocked me down with a feather when I got a filming schedule. Fuck me – this was actually happening. Millions of dollars were being spent and actors were being hired – and there we all were in Petaluma.

I can only describe it as a surreal experience. The rapper Chris 'Ludacris' Bridges was there. He told me that as soon as he saw the script and heard about my life, he made sure he was part of the movie. That really hit home with me as I'm a big film buff and this is a guy who was in *Crash*, which won three Oscars. He's no joke and that's not even mentioning his work in the *Fast & Furious* films. Ludacris was cast as my dad, Eldridge.

Sasha Alexander plays my mum Marianna, while Christina Moore plays my wife and I play my own biological father.

The production team decided that while my real name would be used, my original birth name was switched from John Craig to John McCord. The film obviously had to change some details of my life to make it work visually, but it's about 80 per cent true though. They wanted to include my start in life but we only had the two hours or so of running time.

So my sisters were cut out and they kept it to my brother and I – although he's called Rory in it, not Thomas. I must say that my brother was a real pain in the arse during filming. He wasn't there but I'd added him on to my Facebook so he could see the pictures but he kept leaving annoying comments, pretty much saying something didn't happen or it happened this way, not that way.

One thing in the movie is that my character as a kid gets a swastika tattoo and in my mind, my brother really did try to do that to me by brandishing a needle and some Indian ink. But he flatly refutes that and says it's just a prominent vein at the top of my ear. Either way, more than once I had to remind him it was Hollywood.

Another example is when I have to choose to either stay with my adopted parents or return to my biological parents. I did that in a court but for things to flow better on screen, I make that choice in a restaurant. The way they set the plot in America was actually a joint idea as I'd suggested that my birth dad was portrayed as moving to the States to marry a girl, because I wanted the Scottish element in there. We were never going to get the money or logistics together if we had set it in Scotland as America is where the cash is for this sort of project.

So my biological dad was written as having moved over to marry a woman, and then putting his family through hell – just like in reality. Ali had urged me to take a role as he said it was one of the luxuries of having your life projected to the world, and I shocked them all by saying I wanted to play my biological dad. I hated the man; it wasn't a tribute, I just really didn't think anyone else could get over how much of an asshole he was.

I also wanted it to be real and I wanted every single viewer to really feel it – and okay, I'd done a little bit of filming on the Aussie soap *Neighbours*, but I'd never have the gall to say I was an actor. But I wanted to nail it so I teamed up with Sasha Alexander. She's another big-time operator and I'd seen her on the TV series *NCIS*, but she has also popped up in one of the *Mission Impossible* films. I really have to doff my cap to Sasha as I admitted I was struggling in some ways to summon the rage that my biological dad had inside him. I found it hard to recreate that, even as an act. I mean, we're talking about a guy who treated his sons like punchbags.

Sasha actually had me over at her place and let me practice it as I needed a woman to bring it out of me. I think that's what fuelled my biological father, some sort of hang-up on being a macho man – whatever the fuck that meant to him. He always had to be what he thought was strong and powerful. So Sasha goaded me and made 'me' a lesser man, and I was using his headspace.

It was powerful stuff; I really felt him leap out and appear like a genie in a bottle and it was also one of the oddest experiences of my life. There I was on the sofa getting seriously deep emotionally with Sophia Loren's daughter-in-law. Sasha and I have got a bond, and without name-dropping she is good friends with Ewan McGregor and Robert Downey Junior.

So she'd suggested that we all have a dinner party. I tried not to give a direct answer, as how am I going to look sitting there in between Obi-Wan Kenobi and Ironman?

I have to say that on the day, I did find that the filming was hell and I couldn't have done it without Sasha's sessions. I was Thomas Craig S1enior – Ewan

McCord on screen – for ten hours and it was a disgusting experience. I realised it was necessary for people to watch the movie and learn lessons. But I hated it – I felt like I needed a shower when the director finally called 'cut' for the last time.

The other actors and extras were also a bit standoffish as they didn't think I'd dig that deep. Maybe some had assumed my tales of what he was like were an exaggeration, but they saw it that day.

It wasn't a smooth process for the crew as I struggled to get his essence. I really found it hard being that nasty and abusive in front of a load of folk, including my new girlfriend Nikki, who joined me on set, and some lines took 15 takes. Even the night before, we had a bit of a panic as I was told I was playing Thomas as an American, but I'd spent all my time practising as a Glaswegian. I had to plead with the producer Hadeel that I really needed to do it in a Scots brogue as my poor attempts at an angry American ended up sounding like a camp Texan. Ali weighed in on my side so at least I didn't have any accent worries.

It was purely about forcing myself into his mindset and when I finally got there, I wasn't proud I managed to nail it – it was more of a necessary evil. One really positive note about the actual filming process was that we spent a week at a juvenile detention centre as it doubled as my children's home Glenrosa – and the kids who went there got the chance to take on small roles.

I really enjoyed being around them, even though I'd not been in any place like that since I was adopted. I remember one wee lad in particular, his mum was there as we needed adult supervision because they were minors, and he was full of rage about how his stepdad was an asshole. So I took him to the side and said, 'Look wee man, I've been there and you'll put all this shit behind you, just don't stop believing.'

The mother ended up in tears and we all had a big hug and that's really what I want to do with this movie. I don't care who knows that I sold the rights to my story for $1 and I didn't even get that – as the cheque is sitting on my mantlepiece and I won't ever be cashing it. I did work as an associate producer, helped out the athletes and planned out bike stunts, so I had a day to day role but my main aim is to reach just one kid out there.

Whether he or she is from Africa, Austria or Antarctica, I just want to show them – you're not your past. No matter how bad a hand you get dealt, no matter how much people mistreat you – you can forge your own path.

To someone that might mean becoming a rock star; to others, it must be securing a steady job flipping burgers. The struggle is between your ears and if you're happy and can look yourself in the mirror, and say 'I'm living the way I want to' then you're golden and that's all I want any kid to take from the movie, or this book. Strip away all the glitz and glamour, my message is this

– you're not a product of your environment, and only you can choose who you're going to be today.

And the biggest nod to that I got was from the big boss himself, Steven Spielberg. As *ET* is so central to my whole BMX journey, the production team wanted to recreate the scene where young John sits down and is encapsulated by seeing the bike for the first time. A message was sent over to Spielberg's studio as he needed to sign off on it personally. Nothing was coming back so Hadeel took the bull by the horns and just went over. Somehow she got in a room with him and managed to get the great man to watch some scenes from the movie. He bloody loved my story, he reckoned it was seriously good and gave the green light to include the clip. I mean, what the fuck – I was pogoing around my living room when they told me that. Spielberg knows who I am and likes my story, what a ride!

Every part of the movie process has seen me get further and further up Everest and I've been high on life since moving to America, but the last few years have been a mind-bending trip. I don't know what they smoke in the jungles of Bolivia but I fucking know what it feels like now.

One of my best memories when I see the movie – it'll be released in 2018 – now is how I mentored Shane Graham playing me, John Buultjens. That's a ridiculous thing to write as the guy is box office – he's going places in the business but as he was playing me, we worked really closely and he picked up all manner of things from me. The best element is my swagger as Glasgow is a city that manufactures a certain type of man who has it; the kind of guy who'll start a brawl over a tiny incident and they carry it a certain way. You know if you want it, you can get it.

I had that as a youngster as to be fair, if you wanted it, you got it – just like the guy at Saint Charles' Primary School who got it from me when I cracked open the bridge of his nose. My fucking biological father would have got it if I'd got closer to him with that kitchen knife but he knocked me out. It was only my dad Eldridge who stopped it, he gave me lessons on how to walk properly, to stop this striding about like I was a fucking hard man ready to rumble.

So I was really impressed with Shane's approach. He had looked into the Glasgow wide-man thing and found out about the walk. He really had it down pat and then he passed it on to Alexander Davis, who plays me as a nine-year-old. Alexander was amazing and how he was able to get the emotions over on camera was beyond me, especially for someone so young, and I even found some of his shoots distressing so had to step away. I was watching myself go through the tortures of my childhood for real. It was not something I expected to affect me, but it did.

Anyway, I spotted Shane one day so passed the swagger thing on to him and it made sense as that little bit of continuity would work brilliantly. It was a subtle thing that the real film aficionados would spot. Magic stuff – but it was only when Shane told him something along the lines of 'just watch John as he walks, study it and copy it'.

I burst into laughter and the two of them looked at me puzzled. I was almost on the floor, wheezing away, and I had to put them straight.

I don't have the swagger anymore. I only walk this way now because I've got one leg shorter than the other! That was from a big crash and all the surgeries during my career but you couldn't have made it up, it was hilarious.

Another thing in the movie beyond my wildest dreams was the contest scene. It is a bit like *The X Factor* or *American Idol* as young John enters a competition, eager to show off his BMX skills.

And I hit upon the idea for my heroes, the 1980s superstars, to be the guest judges. I figured if one of them agreed then that would be really cool – and give the BMXers watching a famous face to marvel at.

But stop the press, they all agreed. I'm pretty close to Brian Blyther, Mike Dominguez, Ron Wilkerson and Xavier Mendez so I asked all of them, but I really wanted to get Mat Hoffman to complete the set – all the original legends in one movie scene, playing themselves.

Mike Escamilla knows him better than me and plays the contest announcer – but actually is a mover in the stunt world as he had just wrapped up on *Guardians of the Galaxy Vol. 2*. So via him, Mat rang me.

He told me about how he never knew my past and all the things that had gone on, and that he'd be honoured to get involved. What a buzz to have all my heroes playing themselves in the movie about my life.

Word really spread through the BMX world and the film has really cemented my reputation as being the bridge between the current scene and the 1980s glory days.

Robbie Maddison was also keen to be part of it. He called me and referred to me as 'the famous Scottish John'. This is a guy who's got millions of fans and the only thing that stopped him joining us on set was that he had another one of his spectacular stunts to film in Tahiti at the same time.

But it even got to the point that I was turning riders and actors down, not because I didn't rate them but just there were no other parts to play. It only really hit me how far I'd come when on one of the final days, we were up in Napa Valley at the skatepark there filming the contest scenes with the judges. I walked over and Mike and Mat were chattering away – and Mike was telling Mat to repeat back what he had just said.

Mat was a bit shy as he is a humble dude and didn't want to come over wrongly or bitter in any way – which he isn't. Finally he opened up and told me that he'd created over 100 tricks, wowed people all over the world and nearly died on his bike, but I'd attacked my dad with a kitchen knife and got a movie made about me! We all burst out laughing and I hugged Mat, telling him he has always been and will always be a hero to me.

I don't think I'll ever get used to the fact that my crazy experiences, daft jokes, mistakes and triumphs will be around forever thanks to my own Hollywood movie.

Not bad for a kid from Whiteinch – and the best thing is I'm showing everybody else out there what BMX is all about.

All my circle is hardcore about the sport, but I know 99 per cent of the people in cinemas or who get it on DVD or download it online won't be. I'm proud as punch to be passing on the torch for the sport that's given me everything.

And I only want one message to be left behind when the credits have rolled and the screen goes black.

You're not your past – and always keep chasing your dreams.

# 19

# Dear John

DEAR John Craig,

I wanted to reach out to you as you've sadly not had anyone show you the way forward in life.

You're stuck in a hellish situation.

You're used to violence and hatred surrounding you.

It's not your fault and none of it is your doing.

But you won't be able to comprehend that at five years old.

You've been bombarded with mixed messages, by witnessing lots of inappropriate behaviour and turmoil.

You're about to be given away by your mother.

That's not going to be easy to take and will leave your young mind all over the place.

But you have to keep believing.

Things can change in the blink of an eye.

A lot of cynical adults will tell you that you can't change, that if you're born into a certain background your potential is capped.

But I'm telling you from experience, that's not the case.

A glass ceiling is only there for one reason – and that's to be shattered.

So just keep your mind and heart open.

Don't reject people or let things from the past torture you.

If they do, take a deep breath and focus on what you can do, not what you have done.

Shoot for the moon and you might just reach the stars.

You might even make the moon too.

Nothing is stronger than a positive mindset and a desire to improve.

You can do it.

Live in the present and leave the past where it belongs.

I know you can – because I did.

Always and forever,

John Buultjens (2017)

# Index